Wanting Becoming Believing

Wanting Becoming Believing

Wanting can be an act of faith by which we find God.

William Lucian Joiner

Judson Press ® Valley Forge

Wanting, Becoming, Believing

Library of Congress Cataloging in Publication Data

Joiner, William Lucian,
Wanting, becoming, believing.

Includes bibliographical references.
1. Christian life—1960- I. Title.
BV4501.2.J584 248.4 80-21266
ISBN 0-8170-0884-5

Printed in the U.S.A.

For Barbara,
my wife,
the most significant person
in my wanting

Some Contributions to Acknowledge

Others have been instrumental in the completion of this book, and I want to express thanks to them. They have been the inspirers, encouragers, advisors, and loyal critics.

Al Pope, friend and colleague, grew a beard. It became the focus for one of his sermons, the gist of which was: What have *you* always wanted to do? Perhaps it is a clue for God's will for your life. Al's sermon is the kernel of truth which I have sought to expand in this book.

Betsy Spriggs, career counselor, helped me sort through what I wanted. During a down time in the writing of this book, when she suggested that I possibly didn't want to write at all, my anger created energies for sorting quickly through priorities. Investing again in *Wanting, Becoming, Believing* put other energies back to work.

Harold Twiss and Cynthia Mooney have been patient and gentle in their editorial suggestions and questions. The language has been made more accurate and the thought sharpened by their careful work.

Barbara Bell, typist *extraordinaire,* labored with grace and determination through my rough drafts. Her patient deciphering of a combination of typing and writing was a solid contribution to this book.

For whatever does not track, won't wash, and seems hazy as morning fog the author claims exclusive credit.

William Lucian Joiner

Contents

Introduction

This business of wanting is like playing with matches—you'll probably get burned. For that reason we are more comfortable with what we *ought* to do, *ought* to feel, even what we *ought* to want.

It is as if some inner censor has made us feel that what we want cannot really be good. As one of the graffiti sayings has it, "Everything I want is either illegal, immoral, or fattening." On the other hand, there is the feeling that what is good must taste bad and/or be a nasty ache in the conscience.

So then if our wants are to be baptized and we become praying persons, we must stretch our wants beyond delight and fasten them onto discipline. And what we usually mean by discipline is eating the spinach of life just because it is good for us.

Jack Jackworthy runs every day, rain or shine, through cold and snow, a kind of postal loyalty the postal service itself has forgotten. He dresses up in a ridiculous outfit, his head covered with his jersey's hood, his gym pants as baggy and pegged as a 1942 zoot suit's britches. With his very athletic shoes, he charges out to run through the neighborhood to the yapping of the dogs. It is not that he gets a bang out of it. On a pleasure scale of 1 to 10, it rates about minus 3. So why all this puffing and blowing drudgery? Because it is fun? Pleasurable? Enjoyable? No. BECAUSE IT IS GOOD FOR HIM.

Here's hoping it enables Jack to live long enough to find something enjoyable, with fun to it. May he live to do something he wants—not because it is good for him—but because he wants to do it.

But, if in order for all our wants to become good (or at least, harmless) they must be distilled into a spinach-and-jogging thing, then what's the use of spinach and jogging? If it's all to be determined by what's good for us, then when do we get to use this disciplined mind and body for what is fun and pleasurable, for what is exciting and enticing, for what is delightful and charming? What place shall wanting have in our living? Where is wanting in the hierarchy of our priorities?

In order to get to whatever we want, there is obviously a price to be paid, and that price has some spinach and aching muscles to it. Yet surely what we pay ought to bring us something of what we want. And what we want ought to be more than what someone has determined to be good for us.

Most of the time religion has been assumed to be a nasty-tasting experience which some undergo in order to discipline themselves. One tries to be religious because it is one of those spinach-and-jogging things. Faith is supposed to be made up of such aching exercises as duty, repression, judgment, and ritual.

It would be a very different "do" if religion had to do with enhancing and encouraging wanting. Now, that would blow your whole mind, heart, soul, and strength! It fairly stretches the imagination out of shape. Religion becomes no longer a no-no, but a resounding yes-yes. It gets saved and converted from a narrow, condemning life to a bright, broad affirming one. It gives up its fears generated by repressiveness and is regenerated into blowing the lid off. It would begin not with what I must do; it would rather start with asking (as if it were really interested), "What do you want? How can I help?"

Is all that too marvelous even for the miracle makers? Can the real nature of religion actually begin with what I want?

The object of this book is to examine our wanting, our faith, and the relation between the two.

It is my conviction that the relationship is a real one and that one is the *sine qua non* of the other; one is yin and the other yang, alpha and omega, left and right.

Religion is the expression of our faith, or, at least, of something that passes for that faith. My contention is that our religion becomes more genuine, more consistent with our faith as we are aware of the meaning of our wants. In fact, I am suggesting that the beginning point for our faith is not what comes to us from the outside of us as if to fill some unbelieving gap in our souls. Faith is born inside us. To borrow Paul Tillich's favorite term for faith, it is our "ultimate concern." It is that which matters above everything else. The beginning point for "ultimate concern" is in the wells of our wants. Therefore, to want, to become aware of what we want, to know the meaning and consequences of our wanting is a profound act of faith.

William Lucian Joiner

Yes?

"Our Father who art in heaven, hallow—"

"Yes?"

"Wha—?" I looked around the room. No one was there. The shade flapped in the breeze at the window. It was dark outside, quiet and still. I listened. Nothing. I started again:

"Our Father who art in hea—"

"Yes?"

"Who's there? What do you want?"

"Who's there? It's your 'Father in heaven'—although more accurately, your 'Father *from* heaven.'"

I jumped up as if some shot of electricity had energized my stand-up mechanism. There was nothing, nobody. Still the shade flapped in the window. I looked outside. Nothing. Only the pitch black of night. I closed the window. I wasn't deranged. I had heard a voice, distinctly. I looked at the door and barked in a commanding tone: "What do you want?"

"What do *I* want? I thought the real reason for praying was for you to tell me what *you* want. Did you really call your 'Father in heaven' to ask me what I wanted?"

The voice didn't come from anywhere; it came from everywhere. It was not from the door, the window, or anywhere. It sort of surrounded me; it had no identifiable source. It was not above, not below, not left or right. It just *was*.

Then the words began to soak in.

"Well, uh, yes, Sir. I mean, what you want, uh, Thou want, I mean wantest, uh . . ."

"You. Say 'you.' If only people knew how ridiculous they sound, trying to speak seventeenth-century language to me. Now what can I do for you? Why did you call me?"

"Well, uh, Sir. I didn't really call Thou, uh, you."

"Weren't you praying?"

"Well, yes. Uh, as a matter of fact, I was."

"So?"

"Sir?"

"What do you want? What can I do for you?"

"Want? I guess, uh, I don't know. I was just saying my prayers. No, Sir, I don't know what I want."

"I'm sorry. If you find out, call me back."

"Oh, yes, Sir, I will."

"And, Joe—"

"Yes, Sir."

"I love you. S'long."

I turned and looked toward the window. The shade hung limp and still. It was all quiet again.

1 Wanting and Believing Were Made for Each Other

Touching the Christian faith ever so lightly, one might assume that to be a successful Christian means to have found a workable way to have squelched all wants. The ever-ready, fully automatic Christian has the skill and tools to put the lid on all urges, desires, and wants. In short, since wants are the source of temptation, and temptation, if not short-circuited, produces sin, wants have to be controlled like a tiger in the zoo. (A zoo is a better analogy than the circus because tigers perform in a circus, even though they are controlled by whip and cage. It's safer simply to look at a tiger behind bars, wasting away into impotency, than to be disturbed with any display of power.)

Is this the faith for the followers of Jesus of Nazareth? The record of what he said and did, the New Testament, seems at points to say that wanting *is* bad business. It *seems* to be saying that what we are to want is what God wants, so that the circuits that carry our wants into consciousness and into action are to be turned off. God's wants (sometimes known as "the will of God") are to be turned on and left on.

For instance, look at Matthew 6:10. It is part of the prayer that Jesus gave his disciples, and it is assumed that a disciple will be praying in the spirit of this prayer. The prayer says in part: "Thy kingdom come, Thy will be done, on earth as it is in heaven."

"As it is in heaven." That's got to be complete, without compromise, definite and constant. When the Lord says, "Sing, Angel," the angel does not offer excuses about talents or complain about being busy. The angel simply says, "Yes, Lord, what number?" God wants it done; it happens. And that's that. ". . . Thy will be done, on earth as it is heaven."

That seems specific enough. There's too much fighting and bickering going on down here. Somebody's got to get it straight, somebody with the power to impose his or her will. There is the source (perhaps the only source) of law and order.

Some have felt that they knew what the will of God was; so they gathered whatever power they could in order to see that it was done, and done right. To God be the glory! They made laws about Sunday closing for all businesses, laws about what books could be sold, laws about what expressions of religion could be tolerated. What, after all, could be nobler than to know God's will and to put the force of law behind it? To wit, to make of this kingdom the kingdom of God where God's will was done to perfection?

Is that what Jesus had in mind?

I suspect that it was something quite different.

From the beginning of the Bible to its ending, the message is that God wants relationships with these creatures, created in the divine image. God pays exorbitant prices for those relationships. The Lord is jilted by the covenant people, like Gomer casting Hosea aside! (Hosea 2:5). The Lord is angered at their lack of trust, cut to the quick by their disregard for justice and equality, the cornerstones of any relationship. The biblical writers experienced their God as one who wanted to know and be known.

"Thy will be done . . ." is a prayer for a relationship to happen in the knowledge of what the Lord God wants. To put it another way, "Let us know what you want, Lord."

Something meaningful is revealed when one lets another know what is wanted, desired, hoped for. That's the time you learn something of another's values. What someone wants hints strongly at one's reason for living. And if you become part of that wanting system, then the relationship is already moving toward intimacy.

Take Joe and me, for instance. I had known there was a Joe for a long time. But he went to Third Ward School and I went to Fourth. Then came the high school years when all the kids from all the wards were poured into one school, like four quarts emptied into a gallon jug. That's when I got to know Joe. I found out what he wanted. He wanted Gwen, mostly, but he also wanted to be a lifeguard at the pool; he wanted to be the best jitterbug (and was) in the class. A whole complex of wants and hopes made up my friend, Joe. When I got to know about those wants and what they meant to Joe, then I knew Joe.

But only knowing what Joe was after might have left me with a bundle of information from which I could compile a biography. That didn't occur to me; that wasn't what I wanted. I wanted a friend, a relationship. That could only come about as Joe knew about my wants and wishes. It was important, too, that each of us knew what the other wanted of the other, that is, how we each fit into the other's complex of wants and goals.

Jesus' prayer is a request for revelation. "Let your will be done" is a way of getting to know what this God wants—what is expected from us. Then the relationship can begin. We will know then what God wants of us, what God's desires are. It is then that we can determine whether or not this kind of relationship is actually possible for us.

When we know that what the Lord God wants has some meaning for us as individuals, we can become trusting enough to share our wanting, also.

But, read on in the same sermon; Jesus gives what seems to be a stern warning: "'Not every one who says to me, "Lord, Lord," shall enter the kingdom of heaven, but he who does the will of my Father who is in heaven'" (Matthew 7:21). That has that navy loudspeaker feeling to it. It is one-way communication. Now hear this! Then follow the orders from headquarters. They are not to be questioned, but carried out. Never mind understanding the commander; just understand and do what has been commanded. There is no relationship to that. We would become God's functionaries, tools to get the job done while the Lord God remains aloof and perhaps unmindful of us and our condition. The job's the thing. If you want a ticket into the kingdom, get the job done. The matter of relationships, fellowship, dealing with your loneliness is an after-hours concern. For now, do what the Boss ordered.

But, is God looking for automatons to carry out holy wants, unfeeling, computer-type individuals who never reason why, but move with mechanical determination to do it (whatever the "it" is)? Surely Jeremiah had a different idea of God and of our relationship to the Lord. To Jeremiah, God was tender, gentle, and longed to be known and to give gifts to the people.

"Is Ephraim my dear son?
Is he my darling child?
For as often as I speak against him,
I do remember him still.
Therefore, my heart yearns for him;
I will surely have mercy on him,"
says the LORD.
—Jeremiah 31:20

Yet there cannot be much (if any) relationship if one disregards another's wants. If we are not God's butlers who look toward heaven and ask, "You rang, Sir?", neither is God our butler. If there is to be a relationship, then we need to take seriously God's desires, wants, will. Jesus is asking, "How can you consider that you are part of God's connection, if you are not interested in God's wants?"

All three of the Synoptic Gospels carry the incident of Jesus' extraordinary demands on anyone who would become his follower. "...'If any man would come after me, let him deny himself and take up his cross and follow me. For whoever would save his life will lose it; and whoever loses his life for my sake and the gospel's will save it'" (Mark 8:34-36).

That's hardly a good text for assertiveness training, for self-actualization therapy. It appears to say that the important concern is not what you want, but how much you give up, and the minimum is everything. It seems to be a Kamikazi recruitment program for the Lord's army. Zoooooooom.... Splash.... Praise the Lord!

There is something gallant about such a sacrifice of one's self, one's life, one's wants, I guess. The urge to be heroic might find some fulfillment here. It is the stuff (some imagine) of which missionaries are made. See what is given up! Family, friends, home, the "good life," and more. But having been part of that selfless society of saints, I can testify to the fact that most of those sacrificing missionaries did not consider that they were giving up anything at all. Indeed, the most effective missionaries always gave the impression that they were doing exactly what they wanted to do, that they found in their work a level of excitement unequaled by anything else they might be doing. Problems? Missionaries were no strangers to tough times. Disappointments came bunched together, and accepting them was always painful. Living as a missionary for three years convinced me that their life was what they wanted, above all else. The problems and disappointments were the inflated price they were willing to pay for the fulfullment of their wants, their wants to give something real to real people with enormous needs.

The whole struggling process of knowing what one wants is the struggle to deny oneself whatever is lesser, whatever conflicts with the primary wants. Priority setting, they call it, and it is not without sweat and tears. Ultimately something has to go. Usually that something is dear and valuable. It is losing part of myself. I grieve at the loss of some of my wants that had become part of myself. Yet I cannot have it all. I am not omnipotent, omniscient, omnipresent. I am a most finite somebody. Limits force me to choose and to lose, lose some lesser concerns to make a try for the primary wants.

Jesus' call to us is to take our wants seriously enough to do the hard work of editing them. And when we have, there will be left over a great mass of wishes, dreams, wants, hopes. It won't be easy to let them go; it will be a painful experience. And it has to be done over and over. The only way these can be let go is by remembering the value and the promise of the primary want(s).

To follow Jesus (to put it simply), we must be convinced that, in comparison to all else, he is worth the loss of all else. We need to be convinced that beyond all these other concerns we want him most of all. That's easy when there is little attachment to "all these other things." But when we are dealing with ideas and life-styles, with dreams and visions of participation in meaningful experiences—all of which are not evil or destructive, but just conflicts—then it is denying self in order to opt for what we want in following Jesus' way. Innocent though some of these concerns may be, they are consigned to the cross and our parting is permanent. Our pilgrimage moves in another way.

To take Jesus seriously in this surrender of self is not to deny our wants; it is precisely the opposite: it is to take them as seriously as we would Jesus' call to discipleship. Whoever doesn't want to be a disciple won't be a disciple. There is no discipleship in name only. We either want it above all else, or we will have other interests. We have already seen that this "Lord, Lord" stuff won't do.

If a superficial reading of the Bible would lead one to conclude that wanting is closer to sin than to an act of faith, a misunderstanding of the church can make it appear that the church's purpose is to get us to deny our wants. Whether or not the church is involved in an active, meaningful mission, the big push seems to be to transfer individual wanting to the needs and goals of the church.

With a hurting group of people, smarting from their guilt, the church can find ready pickin's for meeting their (the church's) needs. The cash flow will improve if conscience-aching people see that giving is a way to deal with guilt.

Besides money, there's the concern about time. Since the church is a volunteer organization, there is always the need to get someone to do something if the program is not to wash out. So the church offers another way to deal with our sense of throbbing guilt.

The giving of money and time may be "grudgingly and of necessity," but it provides the finances and the muscle to get things done. It is another dimension to wanting. Possibly church giving and working is somewhat less than the will of God. It is, most often, not the will, the wanting of the givers and workers.

Lily (I'll call her that) came to my study one day to complain about her husband's strong objections to her working in the church. Lily was a Sunday school teacher, an officer in the women's society; she sang in the choir, was on several committees, and generally was to be found puttering around the church almost any time. "My husband," she complained, "does not understand what it means to be dedicated to the church." For him, her church involvement meant evenings alone, extra baby-sitting, and an absentee wife. "He even begrudges what I give to the church," she said.

Lily was in a serious phase of "churchaholism." She was an addict who needed to let go of the church and begin to discover just what she really wanted in her life. In order to do that, she needed affirmation from some other sources, "permission," the transactionalists call it. Lily needed permisison to want—to see what her wants were saying about the directions for her life. It was time for the church to quit using her and help her find the freedom to want.

But very few churches seem to have learned to reward wanting on the part of their people. Wanting may even seem dangerous, and to reward wanting may feel like signing a blank check, an opening of Pandora's box. All kinds of strange things might happen if the church began to encourage people to look seriously at their wants and to act on them. What sort of latent hostility might be hidden under those smiling faces? The specters of greed might leave the church's coffers emptier than they are. Such encouragement, one might feel, would be to opt for the downfall of people and church.

From the current trend of churches it is not likely that they will be in any danger of incurring such liabilities as would come from church folk finding out about their wants. There is little to indicate that churches are about to reward any other behavior than they have in the past—giving instead of receiving, humility instead of affirmation, sacrifice instead of achievement and fulfillment.

But it is sometimes in just such unlikely circumstances that the trends somehow get put into reverse, and the unexpected happens. After all, for those of us who dare confess we are middle-aged, our history ought to have taught us to expect the unexpected.

Let me at least propose the unexpected: perhaps we can come to terms with our wanting, not only in the church (that would be bold enough) but also *because* of the church. What better place is there? And what better support could we hope for?

If I am right, the Bible has God saying, "I want a relationship with you, and I have taken the first step by sharing my wants with you." Then *we* need to take the next step and share our wants. Yes, of course, the Lord already knows what they are. God knows everything, but I am willing to bet that we have a great deal of ignorance about our own wants. I don't mean that Sid is ignorant of what Sam wants (though that's quite probable). I'm betting that Sid doesn't know Sid's wants, and Sam is unaware of his own wants.

It all is part of the pattern of our living. We are so busy being busy, and we have believed that our wants, if we fooled with them very much, would soon consume us. So we have pushed them out of the windshield view of our awareness. But ignoring them does not evaporate them; they are still very much with us. I am suggesting that the church could become an appropriate setting for Sid to get acquainted with Sid's wants and for Sam to learn about his own. Not only will they both be the wiser about themselves, but, if they share their wantings, their own relationship will be moved to a more meaningful level.

Such a level might begin to happen in churches if they were willing to ask, seriously, some "what if" questions. These questions can become a process for assessing possibilities for the churches to do a more thorough job in their calling to enable people to experience more of their humanness. Let's take a look at the "what if" process and the experience of wanting in relation to the life of the church.

What if, in the midst of the churches' current search to define themselves in terms of fellowship, they understood fellowship to mean a genuine and in-depth caring about one another? Ought not "fellowship" in the church to mean something vastly more important than ham suppers, chitchat conversations, and rousing choruses of "Bringing in the Sheaves"? More than a celebration of all those safe concerns where we agree, are alike, or have similar tastes, we need a kind of respect that allows for all those differences that are often uncomfortable, but more often not understood. If fellowship in churches is to meet human need at profound levels, it must move beyond the obsession with safety.

What if we respected one another and trusted one another, so that we could hear, with genuine respect for the person, all those wants that are not our wants, but which are the wants, wishes, dreams, and passions that come out of the deep end of another's soul?

What if caring were not to lay on each other some safe "oughts" and "shoulds," but to know each other's wants at whatever depth one is willing to share them? In other days, there were single standards for conduct among church folk. If some brother or sister was not fulfilling the single standards, a committee of pastor and deacons came to get the wayward saint back under his or her halo. If the committee members met with refusal, they reported their efforts to the church, and it was left up to the church to decide what to do. Many churches with ancient records have evidence that the decision for the nonconformers was to boot them out; "withdraw fellowship" was the euphemism.

Part of our itchiness and twitchiness now is because the one standard no longer exists, and there is no measure by which to test tolerable behavior in the church. Perhaps we could learn to listen to anything—barring the tearing up of property and hurting people. It would be a step toward taking people seriously, perhaps more seriously than they have been able to take themselves.

What if such listening to one another's wants were more than simply hearing each other's words, but were instead experiencing what another has invested in his or her dreams? What if it were to sense the feelings involved in his or her dreams? What if it were to be really present without the mind wandering all over one's own hungers and urges?

Brad is a good listener. When he hears you, it is as if everything else has somehow gotten frozen in time, and you are the only thawed thing in his life. He drinks your words in so that the line between him and you gets hazy, and he seems to become part of you in a most supportive and affirming way. He is no psychiatrist, no social worker, no counselor. He is a friend who cares and who seems to have no need to assess, judge, evaluate. He is a model of possibility for fellowship in churches. Brad listens to wants as if they were neither good nor bad, but glimpses of a self, and he handles that self with care and respect.

What if the church understood fellowship in terms of in-depth caring?

What if that caring were not to pick at another's peccadilloes, but to listen to anything?

What if such caring were not withdrawal from our differences, but were, instead, seeking to understand in all their dimensions one's wants?

What if? Indeed!

We would probably find ourselves and our fellowships moving toward some new, promising, and fascinating possibilities. More than tromping over well-worn and monotonous paths, we'd be cutting new ones with all the excitement of exploring, of going where we had never been. We would know one another by our wants (among other concerns); and if we refused the temptation to categorize each other by our wants, we would always be discovering people who are different, fun, exciting.

We would also be creating the sort of environment in our churches that encourages honest being. No one would have to test out the way the wind was blowing in order to buy some sort of acceptance. "In that church you'll have to wear jacket and tie, dress and high heels." We need to put over our doors (better, in our minds): "All you who enter this place may be yourselves."

We would be making of the church a place of encouragement and hoping, of strength and support.

Tuesday was group day. I didn't want to go. My anxiety had me tied in gut-painful knots. I passed by the house once. The cars were there. It was not called off. They were all there. I knew there would be no place to hide. They would pick up my feelings as soon as I said, "Hi." They would leave me alone if I asked for it, and that was the sharp edge to my ambivalence. I turned around and went in. Greetings were short, but warm. I sat down, silent. I felt everyone focused on me. I drew a deep breath and began to let it all out.

Frustrations. Failure. Loneliness. It was a throbbing, hurting experience. I began to cry, uncontrollably—deep sobs, shoulders shaking, the whole thing. After I got it all out, when the group began to come back into focus, through watery eyes, someone suggested that we stand up in a circle. I was put in the middle, and for some unmeasurable time, they all stood close and held me, giving me strength, embracing me, holding me up.

That might be a different ball game for most churches—supporting the wants and needs of each other, like that. It may sound strange and weird, radical, trendy—all that. Is it? No one thinks it strange when there is a prayer request in the church: Mrs. Jenkins' nephew is to have surgery tomorrow. Tom McDermitt's father died and the family needs our prayers. Why not a prayer with support and caring for Minnie, because she wants to do a great job on a paper due next week? And for Harold, who wants to begin a new account with a prospective customer he has been developing?

Someone (a nutritionist, I suspect) has claimed that we are what we eat. Perhaps. It might also be said that we become what we want. If we don't know what we want, then we shall become what we don't know.

If the church supported us in our need to know what we want, rather than supporting us in our need to hide from our wants; if the church helped us share our wanting, rather than making us feel greedy for having wants; if the church prayed with us for what we consider to be important goals—then we would begin to discover that our faith begins not with our "oughts," but with our own wants.

Before Christmas

"Twas a while before Christmas," and I sat in my house reading the daily gazette. Noadie sat across from me and had put down her section of the paper. She was staring out blankly into the night. I was vaguely conscious of her and was very aware that she was about to say something. I kept reading faster and faster until my eyes were just skipping across whole lines, but picking up nothing. I wanted to get as much read as possible before. . . .

"Sam."

Too late. "Yes, Love?"

She was still looking out the window. "What do you want for Christmas?"

Hiding behind the paper, I answered, "Oh, well . . . hmmm . . . how about a pair of mismatched sox, an old tire, and two antique mousetraps?"

"Sam! Put that newspaper down and listen to me!"

I peered around the "New Goals for a New America" editorial. "What's putting the newspaper down got to do with listening?"

"Sam!"

I put it down.

Then came that staccato emphasis on each word that implied the message had to be hammered into my head.

Now, face to face. *"What-do-you-want-for-Christmas?"*

"A jug of wine, a loaf of bread—and thou beside me . . . in the bed."

"Wilderness! It's supposed to be wilderness. You know what, Sam, I think you have to be the big man around here all the time. Too big to accept a gift. You have to laugh it off. Oh, well. . . ." She left the room.

From the kitchen: "Want a cold drink?"

"Yeah."

2 Serious Wanting Means Receiving

If the church calendar carried a notice that a prayer meeting was scheduled for next Wednesday, it would feel familiar and right. The church has been praying for a long time, and "to hold prayer meeting" is an expected event. But a Want Meeting?

Monday, 7:30 P.M.—The Board of Deacons will have regular monthly meeting.
Tuesday, 3:30 P.M.—The Annie Duncan circle will meet at the home of Mrs. Maude Trelch.
Wednesday, 7:30 P.M.—The weekly Want Meeting will be held in the church parlor.
Thursday, 7:00 P.M.—The Chancel Choir will practice. Those interested in singing in the choir are encouraged to attend.

What?

A kindergarten exercise: From the above, pick out the activity that is not part of the church's regular life.

The weekly Want Meeting?

Right!

And yet—is that really different from the old nostalgia-covered prayer meeting? What else did we meet for in those days but to share wants with each other and with God? Yet there was a sort of unwritten requirement about those wants (which was not what we called them). They had to be unselfish; they had to show real concern for others' problems. If they were in any way personal, they had to deal with whatever gets in the way of my living the "godly life." If I were struggling with dependency on booze, it was perfectly acceptable for me to confess it, admit that I wanted to change, and ask the folks to pray with me for whatever kept me from living up to the Model.

Wanting had its severe limits, and our praying was to be done within those limits. Wanting was not sinful, but it could be a step in that direction. It had the feeling of selfishness and greed about it. Potentially, it was a move away from God's will; so wanting and praying were like fried eggs and vanilla ice cream—not often found in the same bowl.

One reason that wanting has perhaps never "made it" as an act of faith on equal ground with such concerns as praying, reading the Bible, and teaching Sunday school is that wanting always has to do with receiving, that is, if one were serious about his or her wanting. One does not want in order to want; one wants in order to receive. And there's the rub.

"It is more blessed to give than to receive." It must be true; the Bible tells me so. The way that verse often gets heard could be illustrated in a paraphrase: The ones who can really feel good about themselves are the ones who are generous and are always helping someone. Receiving does not bless; when people are concerned about receiving, they are too wrapped up in themselves.

But that is not what it says. That inaccurate paraphrase comes from and feeds the problem of receiving. It is hard to receive; that demands a special grace of humility that is often humiliating. Being brought up on that good old virtue of self-reliance and independence, how can one feel virtuous when one finds oneself on the taking, instead of the giving end?

There are some special problems where receiving is concerned. If we are to begin to ask, seek, and knock, we would do well to look at whatever seems to block our receiving.

Receiving necessities seems to be especially hard. When the stuff received is of the meat-and-'taters variety, then it seems to say that the receiver has not the wit and wisdom, the strength and determination to do what needs to be done for one's self. Receiving under such circumstances as that deeply stings one's sense of adequacy.

After all, if I cannot manage to put the victuals on the table, pay the rent, and keep clothes on the family, then how am I better than the folks I assume to be dull, weak, and lazy? That kind of receiving would smash my self-image like a cheap light bulb in a sudden surge of current.

Mike and Maude (let's call them) were faced with this sort of receiving, and it raised a serious problem for them. It made me hurt with them in their predicament, and I wondered if I would have the grace to react any differently than they did.

It was Christmas, that time when the givers seem to come to life, looking for their portion of that "more blessedness" to be brought on by their giving. In our church we were searching for people who were hard up. There weren't very many in our small village. But there were Mike and Maude. I knew that they would not have a very special Christmas dinner; so I nominated them as recipients of our generosity. There would be eggs, meat, flour, and potatoes, but there would be some delicacies, as well. My wife had baked a little fruitcake for them. It would show our concern and our generosity, and I could imagine Mike's saying, "Well, they sure have their heart in the right place."

So, with the bundle of goodies under arm and with a warm glow of goodness about me, I charged forth on my pious errand.

I was unprepared for my reception. When I got out of my car (which I had fortunately parked at the end of the driveway), a ferocious, teeth-bared German shepherd lunged at me. His rope was only about ten feet too short for him to have had a generous bite out of my leg. He was determined that I was not going to make it to the door. Devout coward that I am, I thanked God for the lack of ten feet of rope, slithered back into the car making placating sounds toward the dog and went on my way. When I called, Maude told me in no uncertain words that they did not want our charity. Things were just fine with them, and I should look for some other family on whom to practice our generosity. The dog, I surmised, was there to protect them from such blessed givers as I.

Admittedly, it was a rather patronizing thing for us to do, but I hurt that Christmas. My turkey didn't taste as good as usual, knowing that Mike and Maude were dining on the simplest fare.

Yet I know it all from their side, too. I have my vicious dogs as well. They are symbolic, of course, but I think their bark is heard. "Don't make me feel like an incapable, inadequate nobody. If you get any closer with that basket, I'll bite you!" It's tough to receive.

It does something to the way I feel about me. All of which makes it even tougher to ask.

Besides the problem of receiving the bare necessities, there is the problem of receiving the favors, the kindnesses that may come our way. That kind of offer can also raise the defenses. What, after all, does the giver expect? If there is an obvious loan, or some payment (in kind, or whatever) expected, then there is no problem. You give; I receive: I give; you receive—case closed. We are back even again. But what if the other end of the giving is unclear? What I may not know is what is expected of me for the favor given. How can I get things back to zero where you don't owe me and I don't owe you?

An invitation comes to spend a weekend with John and Sally at their cottage on the lake. It'd be a blast—they have a beautiful boat, the view is gorgeous, it's off in the woods where there is no intrusion by civilization. Something leaps up in me with uncontrolled enthusiasm. *Wow! Let's go!* Then somebody else in me demands attention, quiets the wild inner kid down, and says, sarcastically, *Just exactly how do you suppose you could ever pay them back for such a weekend? You don't have a cottage; you don't even own a rowboat.*

"Er, John, gee, it looks pretty busy that weekend," I say, as I looked at a perfectly blank calendar. "Maybe some other time." That kid inside me that was so full of excitement now draws me over to a corner where we pout together.

There is the possibility that the giving is the beginning of a relationship. Sometimes the limits of that possible relationship are pretty muddy and uncertain, and that leaves a scary edge to the receiving. *What's Stan after? What does Cynthia really want out of me?*

It would be great (or would it?) if it were all spelled out in as fine a detail as the Book-of-the-Month Club does it. The gift is offered; but before you sign up to receive the gift, read the rest of the application. *Window Washing Made Simple* shipped to you absolutely free when you agree to buy at least four of the book club's selections within the next twelve months. That's definite. I know exactly what's required of me. The limits of the relationship are spelled out in print. No sweat.

But let Dick come by the office with a book, hard-cover, no less.

"Hey, Bill, when I saw this in the bookstore, I thought about you. I want you to have this book. I hope you enjoy it."

I can always manage a gracious sounding, "Well, thanks very much." Dick doesn't hear the conversation inside: *What does this dude want? What does he mean when he saw this book, he thought of me? What sort of somebody does he take me for? What favor is he going to ask of me?*

Then, there is that inner kid again: *Hey, neat! He likes me! He thinks about me. I made an impression on him. I wonder if there are any pictures in the book?*

Relationships sometimes do begin with gifts, and relationships can move toward intimacy and caring, toward honesty and openness. The grace to receive needs to have a courageous side to it, because it just may lead to another way out of the lonely island with the "no gifts" sign on it. But the waters around that island are not only protective, they are also scary.

There's one other concern about receiving: it means someone has guessed something about me, about my likes, needs, wishes, style of living. It is a way of saying, "This is the way I see you." Receiving, then, is not only taking a gift, but it is also accepting someone's opinion of me.

However "unconservative" I may be in other respects, when it comes to clothes, I am a regular reactionary. No bright-colored shirts for me. You can take those loud plaid slacks and . . . you get the picture. It was Christmas (1970, I think). For Christmas Barbara gave me a shirt that had intricate little designs of fiery red and flashy blue vine-like patterns. And there was a tie that matched all this un-me coloring. I kissed her on the cheek and thanked her, but I had to admit later (after the shirt seldom got worn), "Well, it's just not me."

It's really a judgment, I guess. Someone sees me this way or that, and the gift is a symbol of that view of me. Perhaps some see in me what I have not yet discovered. Maybe I really am more than a white- or pale-blue-shirted person. The gift might be a symbol of some potentiality I've put beneath my consciousness. Receiving can be on at least two levels: the gift and the giver's feeling about me. I may have a tough time with both.

I have been concerned in this chapter with receiving things and with whatever the things may symbolize. But receiving is obviously more than accepting things, and the same sort of grace which allows us to accept things might even be stretched to allow us to accept learning from someone.

The writer of Proverbs gets right to the point:

> He who ignores instruction despises himself,
> but he who heeds admonition gains understanding.
> The fear of the LORD is instruction in wisdom,
> and humility goes before honor.
>
> —Proverbs 15:32-33

The dynamics of accepting wisdom or learning is the same as that of receiving other gifts—how I see myself. Am I adequate? Right? Good? Smart?

Learning seems to press for a special receiving grace. The learning that comes out of books is a kind of sneaky learning. Perhaps that's why we are required by law to fess up where we learned our lessons when we dare write for others to view our wisdom.

But to learn from others (as well as from books), from people, persons who may be younger, less educated (at least formally) or less experienced than we—well, now, let's get back to the books. Learning from someone else seems to uncover my ignorance, and I can do without that sort of nudity.

There is a feeling that life has some sort of learning plateau, that there comes a time in which we reach our learning capacity. Past fifty, if I'm ever to reach such a plateau, I'd better be on it now. It's time to be a teacher, not a learner; a giver of wisdom, not a seeker of it. It is time to be the sage, sitting squat-legged on my mountain of experience, of learning, of wisdom. It is time for the eager, young disciples to approach and hear the guru's philosophy, the wise one who has reached the pinnacle of learning.

More likely, such a guru has reached not the pinnacle of learning, but the limits of honesty. That guru must now parade as a person who has learned what gurus need to know. The guru will downplay any further need to receive any new light, because it will call into question the light that has been collected thus far.

There are several ruses that can be used to ward off receiving the gift of learning. It would be nicer to say that they have come from some research I have done, pawing through the library shelves, poring over ponderous tomes of human behavior. The fact is, they come out of experience. I know some of these tactics well, because

I have tried them all. They can work for you, that is, if you want protection from receiving learning. Here they are:

1. *Their concerns are really irrelevant.* There is a double whammy to that tactic: not only is their material meaningless to me, but they are not too bright in supposing that it does have meaning. No one can afford to spend time on the hard business of learning stuff that doesn't mean anything. Time's too short and valuable for that. Besides, it's a mark of my own smartness to be able to assess what is relevant and what is not. It also says that trivia is not my thing. Why, there are all sorts of goodies in that tactic.

2. *They don't know what they're talking about.* There is that part of the old proverb that goes: "He who knows not and knows not that he knows not is a fool. Shun him." Unmasking the pretenders to wisdom and knowledge can be great fun, particularly when there is no risk involved. Millicent wants to go to a marriage enrichment course. Throckmorton wants to relax with that unfailing instrument of learning and educational opportunity, the television. Millie makes her case on the need to grow and learn new things about how to make their marriage really take off on the wings of love. Throck's retort: "Listen, you know that guy running the course? He is divorced. He obviously doesn't know what he's talking about." Or, as someone recently discovered in desert research, you can't draw water from a dry well.

3. *It's a conspiracy.* I was as scared as any freshman when I went off to college. In fact, maybe more so. My pastor had sat me down and told me all the terrible and wicked things I was probably going to get thrown at me, the liberal and modernistic heresies. I was obviously being thrown into a veritable and insatiable maw of conspiracies designed to pollute my morality and dilute my faith. My grades showed how successfully I had defended myself against the onslaught of learning. But in all that experience I at least came out with a successful ruse that will foil learning every time: those people (from whom I might learn) are up to no good; their ways are nefarious; and their ends are wicked. If I accept learning from them, I, too, will be nefarious and wicked.

I suspect there is a whole catalog of ways to protect oneself from learning, from receiving the gift of understanding. I can guarantee that these work; I can also guarantee that they will take from one far more than they can give. If they protect, they also demand, and the demands are disastrously inflated.

I suppose that we feel we need protection from learning because, for many of us, learning is frightening. It has its edge of fear, almost panic. We may feel that without such protection, we may discover that we have been living more by prejudice than knowledge, more by assumptions than by fact. Perhaps the fear is mostly one of change. Life with the old knowledge is comfortable and nonthreatening.

Learning may change our values. That will scare the willies out of us, all right. That comes just too close to having to admit that we have been living by less than real values, or other than real values. Either admission leaves us with the confession that we are not essentially good. Such a confession would be a shattering admission.

This concern was my freshman fear in college. It may have been Throck's fear of the marriage enrichment college, i.e., that he would discover that all along he's been wrong, a rotten husband and miserable lover. Some (maybe most) of that scare is unreal. It doesn't make sense to turn life over to whatever may scare us, letting our fears take control of it all.

Learning is too great a gift from which to hide. It is really a double gift, especially when it is a face-to-face sort of learning, the sort that comes from a relationship. That kind of learning is not only accruing knowledge, but also it is accepting another in a special way. It is affirming the other's gifts. It is allowing that person into one's life on a plane that begins with trust. It is taking another seriously. Two gifts are received in a learning relationship: what another knows and what another is.

No gift is more important and no gift is harder to receive than love. Long ago, back in the days of music, there was a song that apologetically claimed, "I Can't Give You Anything but Love." But it was like a lot of love songs in those days: whoever was supposed to have heard this passionate ditty ought to have had the opportunity to answer. If the reply had been honest, it might have been something like: I can accept anything but love. Passion, possibly. Admiration, oh, yes. Roses and chocolate cherries, sure. But love? Real intimacy? Caring? Commitment? Devotion? Uh, well, that's different, and perhaps the reason that it is different is that the gift of love is only half received if we only take and do not return it.

I love you.

That's dynamite! It's just not possible to drop that one and go away. If it were (maybe like a telegram delivered), it might not be so hard to receive. But love is no telegram; it's not even a message. It is being close, genuinely close. It is far more than rubbing bodies (although embracing and touching are part of it all); it is a closeness that comes from being known openly and honestly; it is finding oneself accepted, even when all the skeletons are out of the closet; it is to experience that one's life is important to another.

That kind of love uncovers the grand ambivalence of life. We want that kind of love, sometimes desperately, but our want has the cold edge of fear to it. That kind of love entices us. We conjure up fantasies of such acceptance in our dry times, but we allow substitutes which are poor imitations of the real hope. Or, perhaps, the fantasy has to do with being acceptable and worthy of admiration, so we can accept all the adulation and praise that the great crowds offer us. Why, we can even enhance the whole scene with a sort of graceful humility about it all: "Aw, shucks, folks."

The great crowds go home. The fantasies end. Slowly we come back to our real world, cold and lonely.

A friend has, in his office, a painting of two people sitting at tables next to each other. One is a young woman who is staring blankly into an empty wine glass. The other is an old man who has apparently finished a meal and he sits looking out into space as if he were not really aware of what he was seeing. Neither has anyone else at the table. The picture has a feeling of desperate loneliness about it. I have thought it would be great to be a waiter in the cafe. I would say, "Hey, Roscoe, have a glass of wine on the house. I want you to meet Jenny. Let me fill up your glass, Jenny." From there on I dream they begin to talk, share life stories, and the loneliness melts away.

Receiving love is more than fantasy, and the difficulty of allowing it to happen has to be dealt with.

What makes it so tough to receive love? Why is it the most difficult of all things to accept?

Receiving the gift of love forces one to deal with the question of one's own worth.

"Why would anyone love me?"

"Why would anyone let me make a difference in his or her life?"

"What is there about me that would make someone care about me?"

It is, perhaps, the chicken-and-egg sort of thing: which must come first—love that will allow me to accept myself or self-acceptance that will allow me to receive love? I shall leave that egg for the philosophers to hatch. I have the feeling that it is love we accept that allows us to believe we are acceptable to be loved. But love is risky business and the uncertainty of it may well leave us at our lonely tables, gazing into our empty wine glasses.

If the risk is too great, we may allow substitutes, some faint hint of love in a safer relationship. The substitutes will be important for us. They may not be the real thing, but they are all we may have. Since they are important—these makeshift concerns—we'll work and sweat to get them, for in some way they will offer the timid, but ambiguous promise that we're OK.

One such substitute is being pleasing to people. Who hasn't played that role on the stage of life at one time or another? With all the real feelings and opinions, beliefs and aims safely hidden from view, we meet another and talk about all those things that don't scare either of us. We feel the way the wind is blowing and try to ape the values we assume we see, in order to earn some acceptance.

Every parent knows that awful pressure that comes when the child comes home and announces, "But everybody else is doing it." Most probably we parents taught them that acceptance comes from doing the "others' things," letting the neighbors or acquaintances set the values, the styles, the patterns of our lives. Why? Because we have this deep hunger of our inwards that prizes being "one of the gang" in the absence of love.

Still further removed from love is that sort of acceptance that comes from being pretty or handsome or sexy. The market is full of all sorts of compounds that can make one absolutely irresistible to the opposite sex. No more of this butting heads together like a couple of bull moose in rut, each trying to crack the other's skull to see if he might win the nearest available female moose. Instead, with the expenditure of a few bucks for the right after-shave, the nearest available female will become helplessly passionate and fall, panting, into one's arms. Potions for luring men into a woman's clutches are even more numerous.

If our society had to do without the assumption that to be sexy is to be real, genuine, complete, we would surely be in an economic depression, and the advertising world as we know it today would cease to exist.

The promise is that anyone can become acceptable if he or she loses weight, if he or she develops a magnificent body with its bulges properly arranged. It is well within the grasp of us all to become attractive and thereby attract the attention we so deeply crave.

Yet, in spite of all the attractiveness that male or female can derive from bottles, tubes, clothes, diets, etc., there is a problem. Once all these magic concoctions win the prize, what about performance? Enter the second phase of the promise of sex as life's fulfillment; how well can you perform? Success is everything. A guy may look athletic, but what can he do on the field? Now it's the publishers' turn to make their mint, not to mention the newest phenomenon: sex clinics. The promise is life's ultimate experience—orgasm. (Each in his or her own way.)

Sex is a gift, it is a gift of God. God put our bodies together so we could have and enjoy orgasm. For enjoyment and pleasure, I am glad for such a gift; it's way out in front of whatever is running second. Being more than halfway to one hundred, I hope God will continue the gift, at least until then. And, as the catch phrase has it, "I'll be careful to give the Lord the praise and thanks for it."

But the fireworks of sex is not the substance of love. Love is more than sex. We know the techniques of becoming sexy; we've read the manuals well, and we know the engineering of successful sex. But with such expertise, it is possible to remain ignorant of intimacy, to be lonely and still to want love. It is easier to accept another body, easier to give one's own, than to receive another self or to give oneself.

To receive another's gift of self, of love, puts one in the position of asking seriously: Who am I? If I am to receive love, I need to ask that question. Yes. Who am I, that I should be loved, that I could accept love? I must admit quite honestly—I don't know; I simply don't know.

I know I am lonely, hungry for friendship, sometimes too willing to compromise and settle for acquaintances, some other somebody who will say "Hi" to me when we meet and give me the feeling that that person has seen me before, somewhere. It might be an extra bonus if I felt my name was remembered, too, as well as what the "somewhere" had been all about.

I am someone without any reason to be loved, not a single one. I have no trophy case for a very simple reason—no trophies! My academic records might best be kept in a safety-deposit box in a Swiss bank, along with a lot of the world's other best kept secrets. I am one with all the beauty that racing fatness and creeping baldness can bestow. Add to that the exciting hair color of gray, a face with a wide-angle jaw, the large economy-size neck, and a chemistry that defies the deodorant industry.

And yet, and yet. . . . Who am I?

I am one who is genuinely and deeply loved, accepted for who I am by One who sees in me what I cannot see in myself—the reason for it all (although I suspect the reason for it all is within this One). That kind of love is difficult to accept, and I know that I must keep working on it all the time, that is, to keep struggling to accept the love the Lord Jesus Christ is offering me.

A great deal of the time he decides to give me that love through another person. If it could only be that quiet, private thing without the messiness of other relationships, a desert experience, hermit-style. Yet the gift keeps coming, wrapped in other people's skin.

I have not earned it. I have not paid for it. I have no worth that intrinsically demands that sort of acceptance. Yet, in the lives of people, God keeps on trying to love me, take me for just the somebody I am. Wouldn't it be great just to throw all risk to the wind and accept every gift of love that comes along? I guess it depends on whether or not I *want* to be loved.

If I did want love, and if I were really aware of that want, how would I ever be able to accept it?

Jesus gives us a clue in his reference to receiving the kingdom of God. He said that the only way to receive the kingdom is like a child (Mark 10:15).

The kind of child I think Jesus was talking about was the one whose life had not yet spoiled the innate ability to receive what was offered. It is that time before the child had laid on him or her the need to repay, when it became a matter of bartering instead of receiving. It is the kind of receiving that has to do with an openness that does not question one's own self-worth, allowing one's arms to open and receive.

Maybe there is a little bit of selfishness to that kind of receiving. After all, we have been brought up to believe that thinking about ourselves is a self-centered and sinful attitude. So we have not learned simply to receive at all, only to swap—your kindness for mine. Received and paid in full. Account closed. Yet there is something pure, good, and thoroughly right about the unspoiled ability to receive and not be diminished by the taking—instead, to be enhanced by it.

Part of our growing up has probably been an intense effort to overcome that kind of receiving without giving, to become what we have called "unselfish." There is a wholesomeness with which a child thinks of himself or herself and is thus allowed to receive.

The child also receives without the need to pore over this act as if it might mean that he or she will always be a receiver and never a giver. A child is not concerned about being caught in some demonic pattern of living from which escape is not possible. The child can trust the good intentions, both of the giver and of himself or herself, and never worry about being able to give.

Perhaps we have been led to believe that it is the one who gives, who shows some measure of success in life, who has some achievements that have brought that person the ability to give. If one has never achieved anything, one cannot give anything. In that frame of reference, receiving may say that one is not adequate, that is, not able to give.

To get all balled up in whether or not receiving makes one more or less adequate is to receive in some way other than that of the child whose receiving mechanism has not worn out.

"Unless you receive the kingdom of God like a little child, you won't get it at all."

But so far, we have been talking about receiving things other than the kingdom of God. The kingdom of God is manifestation of the power of the Lord God on earth. It is leveling the mountains; it is filling up the valleys. It is judgment. It is the appearance of God's power. The moon turns to blood. The sun burns up into a cinder. A new heaven and a new earth come out of a mighty new act of creation. Then the kingdom comes and God's will is done on the earth as it is in heaven. The day of the mighty WOW and the holy whiz-bang!

So, what is all this in regard to our being able to receive?

For all of that you need the gift of a child's ability to receive?

When we talk about the kingdom of God, are we not talking about the rule of love, of its becoming the deciding factor in the affairs of humanity? The kingdom of God is where love is recognized as supreme. It is the recognition of the power of love. It is to realize that it is more powerful than the armaments of nations, than the nuclear generators' output, than the political forces that hold powers of life and death.

"Whoever will receive the kingdom like a little child. . . ."

Can we receive again like a little child receives? Most of us are not little anymore. Those days are lost in the pit that sucks up all time. Could it be that we could recover the childlike attitude that allows us once more to know how to receive?

We need to begin again, all over again. A new start, only a new start, will allow us to receive like a child again, with joy, surprise, and with grace. Jesus told a grown man, "You won't be a part of the kingdom of God unless you start all over again, unless you are born again" (John 3:3, author's paraphrase). If we are to recover the ability of a little child to receive, we must become little children once more. That is what the new birth is all about. To begin again as the little child will recover for us the lost gift of receiving.

It *is* blessed to receive. It is indeed a rare blessing to be able to receive freely. And if we're to be serious about wanting, we must be serious about receiving—things, learning, love, God's kingdom.

What Do You Want to Be?

For Millie, Uncle Roscoe was a mysterious and romantic giant. He stood six-feet-and-some tall, had a coal black mustache, and was almost, but not quite, skinny. He lived a thousand miles away, in Chicago. For a little girl in Belvedere Corners, Alabama, Chicago was a never-never place.

Since Uncle Roscoe only came by about every five years or so, Millie could enhance the mystery of her uncle by imagining all kinds of weird and wonderful things about him.

Her first meeting was when she was six.

Her mother had packaged her in her frilliest pink dress to be presented to His Majesty, Uncle Roscoe. Millie felt shy and unsure. The stiff taffeta of her dress added to the strangeness of the moment.

Millie couldn't notice Uncle Roscoe's being ill at ease, because all of her own feelings were demanding attention.

Roscoe knew he was being awkward, and he didn't like that side of himself. He placed her on his knee, not sure she wouldn't break.

"Uh, well, Millie, what do you want to be when you grow up?"

Uncle Roscoe couldn't have asked a better question. She knew; deep inside she knew.

"A fireman!"

"Isn't that cute, Roscoe?" her mother chimed in. "A girl fireman!" Roscoe hunched his shoulders to signal his so-what feeling.

Another visit came when Millie was eighteen. She had had correspondence with Uncle Roscoe, and there had been really neat gifts in the interim. Right or wrong, she imagined him living the life of a rich bachelor—fast cars and girls who could keep up with the cars, coming to life at night, and hibernating during daylight hours. All that seemed so different from Belvedere Corners.

This time Millie was more comfortable, with her feelings and with her clothes. She had on overalls and a T-shirt. This time it was mother who was uncomfortable, having lost the what-to-wear fight.

Millie dashed into the family room and plopped onto Uncle Roscoe's lap and hugged him. Mother shot a nonseeing look of resignation toward the ceiling. Roscoe smiled and hugged back. Uncle and niece were much more at ease.

"Well, now, the last time you were sitting here you were determined to be a fireman. Remember?" he recalled.

Another look shot at the ceiling and then mother seemed to wilt with a sigh that had no sound.

It was the worst possible question. It was the opening of a door that needed to have remained shut, locked even, if mother and daughter were to abide each other's presence in the space of one house.

"Of course, I remember. And I *am* going to be a fire fighter (she didn't make an issue of the "man" bit). They have this neat three-month course at the Community College, and if I can get accepted and pass, I'll be the first woman in the fire department."

"Roscoe," the collapsed woman was beginning to be put back together by her anger, "please try to talk some sense into your niece's head. Ladies don't become firemen—firepersons, whatever. Where would she sleep when she's on duty?"

"Mother!"

Roscoe said, "Hmmmmmmm."

3 Wanting to Be

Buford (we'll call him) was a straight, crew-cut, former air force officer and an engineer with a super-rational brain. He could almost always cut through all the gray and separate it into its white-and-black components.

I had a problem communicating with Buford. It was almost as if we were speaking two different languages. "Why are you always on this identity crisis stuff? I know who I am. You know who you are. People who don't know who they are have amnesia."

If Buford is right, life would be a whole lot simpler, but it would also be more boring. It is true that a lot of the pain and struggle would be evaporated with the lifting of the "amnesia." But Erik Erikson et al. have helped us to understand that personal identity is as complicated a mechanism as are the electronic machines Buford worked at with great care and patience.[1]

Martin Buber felt that "Who am I?" was actually a religious question. It deals with the most significant relationships in one's life, even those that are beyond the human, the extra-human. That identity is determinative of all our other relationships and significantly governs whether we relate to each other as "Thous" or as "Its."[2]

Freud saw identity as something we soaked up from our authority figures. Their prohibitions and duties were absorbed into our thinking so that we developed this higher "me," this overlord who issues commands and denials. The unique identity, then, is that person that is produced between the overlord and the lusty, vibrant, fun-loving serf who is always ready for a good time. The interplay of these two determines one's character, one's identity.[3]

Variations on these themes bring about endless complications and diversities of our identity.

While I am not in Buford's camp (not entirely), I believe that the complications can overwhelm us, and we can make a career of finding out who we are, endlessly picking at some infinitesimal possibility we may have overlooked. Identity hunting can become an obsession and hide whatever real identity we may have. Somewhere between Buford's simplistic conclusion ("If you want to know who you are, look at your driver's license") and the compulsive reinvestigating of every incident and fiber of one's being, there is a broad outline of an identity that fits, that works, that copes. In that identity our wants and our faith find a common ground.

The Christian faith (among others) asserts that God made us free. We are not, admittedly, completely free. Who could even comprehend what such a perfected freedom would be? Within limits we are free. We are not free to exist forever. There is an end to this thing called life. Mortal, that's who we are, that's our identity. We are smart; but with all our wisdom, we are ignorant. In fact, the honest result of our learning is continually to expose the enormity of our ignorance. We are good; well, we are at least not bad. God only knows if perfection exists and, if so, what it is really like. Our limits in time, intelligence, goodness, etc., are obvious.

We are free, and we are limited. It used to be "in" in theological circles to discover paradoxes. Well, it is surely one to say that we are free, but limited.

Being free (with its admitted limitations) means that we have some choice in our identity, and as soon as we can uncover a choice, we are dealing with our wants. If "Who am I?" was a religious question for Buber, "Who do you want to be?" has equal religious consequences as well.

Tillich spoke of faith as one's "ultimate concern."[4] If one is concerned about who to be, and if one is free (with the limits again) to determine who to become, then the ultimate concern (faith) is a determinative factor in the becoming. That is to say, the degree to which one is concerned about who he or she wants to be, to that degree will one marshal all the resources and plan, work, and struggle to become whoever one feels he or she can be.

I suggest the following as the broad outline of identity of what we want to be. The particulars are obviously left to the individual so that there can be no molds, no assembly-line persons. There may be models, but not molds.

1. We want to be adequate/strong.
2. We want to be good/acceptable.
3. We want to be wise/important.

Let's look at these components.

1. *We want to be adequate/strong.* In the 1940s in many towns, if a boy was not athletic, his masculinity was suspect. He had to get out on the football field and prove his adequacy as a member of the male sex. Knock heads, get mean, show that he could give it and take it. It was mostly brute force. There was some skill involved, but the boy with the skill, but without the strength, was liable to sit dejectedly on the bench and watch. Maleness and strength seemed inseparable, and we boys all wanted to be strong. That would prove that we were men (or at least, reasonably headed in that direction)!

Adler has suggested that the real motivating force in people is power, importance, dominance.[5] It is not enough just to be adequate; one has to be more adequate than someone else, and there is no surer proof of one's adequacy than to be able to tell this man "... Go, and he goeth ... to another, Come, and he cometh ..." (Luke 7:8, KJV). (But, mostly "go to.")

Dreamer Dan (we'll call him that) buys all of this strength/adequacy ideal. In one moment he is the great Arctic explorer, beating the Russians to the South Polar uranium fields. In the next, he is the first trans-Atlantic swimmer, all greased up and swimming in bone-chilling cold. Then he is the world-renowned brain surgeon, in whose hands and skill lay the life of the president. When the bubble bursts, he is once again plain old Dan, taking out the garbage, timidly explaining to the boss why he is late for work, refusing to complain about a neighbor's barking dog. Although Dan never takes the risks that might lead to such superadequacy as his dreams make up, his dreams at least say something about Dan's idea of the strong and adequate of this world.

We are having to wrestle with new ideas of adequacy and strength. Sheer physical prowess may make it on a football field, but the strength we value in our society is usually a different type. It is a strength of character, adequacy of personhood that we call integrity. It is backbone, courage, consistency with one's principles. It is a new sort of strength; it is adequacy in a different dimension.

While brute strength is mostly limited to men (with the exception of some female wrestlers), the new strength is available to men and women. To want to be a person of strong integrity is possible for anyone. Dreamer Dan's fantasies may have included being the most powerful man in the world, but we have sadly learned that the strength of power without the strength of integrity is really weakness and inadequacy.

Integrity is wholeness, completeness. It is that which is not divided, not shattered, not broken. When I look into my inwards, those words don't describe what I see. There is division there, and brokenness and incompleteness. But wholeness is what I want, and I'll probably pay a good price for it, as long as the price doesn't make for more brokenness.

Integrity is honesty. It is not lying, not cheating, not stealing, but it is more, much more. It is the sort of honesty that allows me to confess who I am, without getting it mixed up with who I wish I were. It is also the quality that pushes me to admit what I am and what I am not, in the face of what is expected (or what I conceive to be expected) of me. I like the applause and the you're-one-of-us acceptance from people I value. I get tempted to playact the role that will win the acceptance I want. Then I become a chameleon of uncertain color, changing with the need to be blue to people who like blue, purple for the purple people, etc. I am not a rainbow, and if I am strong enough to be honest, I have to quit "passing" as red when I'm really green at heart.

Integrity is being true to self, a sort of inner consistency. Polonius had good advice for his son: "This above all—to thine own self be true" (*Hamlet,* act 1, sc. 3). There is some considerable distance between Polonius's concern and Narcissus's self-infatuation. The real acceptance is self-acceptance. It means to like the me that I am. It means to care about me, to love me. It is, in Thomas Harris's language, to believe that I am OK.[6] There is a long and unending road between me and perfection, and I know that I am often on some other side road, headed in some other direction. But I am, simply, OK. Perfect? No. But it is OK not to be perfect. It is OK to be the mistake-prone somebody that I am. It is OK not to be superman. To be full of self-reproach, self-rejection, self-doubt is not OK. I would then be against myself—my own enemy, my own Benedict Arnold—a turncoat against me. ". . . to thine own self be true."

So what is this self to which I am to be true-blue? It's full circle: Who am I? I am a wanting one, full of desires to be. I am not done yet, less than fully baked. I know it's OK not to be done yet, not to be finished or perfected. I also know it's OK to want to be more than I am. I want to be strong—and if integrity is strength, I want that.

Meanwhile, back at the paradox place: Whatever did the apostle Paul have in mind when he wrote to the Corinthians: ". . . for when I am weak, then I am strong" (2 Corinthians 12:10)? Weakness is strength? Did double-think arrive two thousand years ahead of George Orwell's 1984 prediction?

Paul believed that strength is not self-generated. Strength, if we have it—of character or muscle—comes to us from outside ourselves. Even the one who is "self-made" makes himself or herself out of something that is not he or she. Strength, then, is dependence. Muscles get strong because we had the right set of genes given to us, because we ate the right foods, inhaled the right air. The strength we have comes from a host of sources on which we are dependent. Strength of character is no less dependent. It is others who make us strong. It is their caring. It is their persistence with us, their patience, their humor, their tears. When we are "strong" enough to admit our weakness, our inadequacies, our loneliness, our needs, then we have set the stage for strength to happen by allowing significant others into ourselves, and in the letting, both the giver and the receiver are stronger.

"When I am weak, then I am strong." I want to be strong, but I must want it enough to become weak—to recognize, confess that I *am* weak. If that confession finds some new strength or adequacy for me out of a significant relationship, then I don't have a blasted thing to brag about, and down deep that feels right. I want that kind of genuine strength.

2. *We want to be good/accepted.*

> Little Jack Horner
>   sat in a corner,
> Eating his Christmas pie.
>
> He stuck in his thumb
>   and pulled out a plum
> And said, "What a good boy am I!"
>
> —Mother Goose

There may be some Mother Goose–Jack Horner types around,

dressed up in their Little Lord Fauntleroy outfits, with hair all slicked down, who feel that they are not only good, but also better than most of us. To use Thomas Harris's language again: "I'm OK, you're not OK." I think they are a rare breed, an endangered species.

Yet I'm guessing that we all want to be good—if not good, at least, not bad. We want to be accepted as good by some standard, by the standard, most probably, set by those who are important to us.

You know you are good in the eyes of your judges when you have been tried and pronounced "cool." You are at last acceptable. You are in. You are good. "Cool," in all its relativity, hardly means Jack Horner. It does mean something about you is OK, and by the standards of whoever the judges might be, you're not bad.

By whatever name—cool, OK, "with it"—we want to be good.

The Pharisees in Jesus' time thought they had discovered the secret of goodness. It was good, old-fashioned (even then) piety. If you do good things, you will become like the things you do—good. Praying is good; so the more praying you do, the better you will become. Fasting is good; so fast a lot and a lot of goodness will happen inside you. Giving the tithe is good; so measure out carefully the tenth part, and, behold, you have bought goodness at the regular (or perhaps even the bargain) price (see Matthew 23: 23).

But the Pharisee always needed a measure for his goodness nearby. He had no way of telling he was good unless there was someone at hand he could outdo in his goodness. He was not convinced he was good until he was convinced he was better than some luckless fellow who had goofed up the piety schedule. The praying Pharisee in the temple thanked God for his goodness, but, oddly enough, his goodness depended on the moral failure of the publican (see Luke 18:9-14).

We seem to need our publicans. Perhaps in our society, the publicans we need are the criminals. They are a ready source of "those we are better than." If we have never murdered, raped, or stolen, we can thank the Lord that we are not like these evil people. We can contrast our goodness with their badness, so that our goodness seems all the better. We may even increase our goodness by judging and condemning the criminals. This is a Jack Horner-thumb-in-the-pie goodness; it is more accurately called self-righteousness. The bitter irony of it all is that that method for producing goodness in us is itself evil. And evil can no more produce goodness than can a tigress give birth to a tree.

If it is true that we all want to be good (by whatever definition), how can we ever be what we want to be?

Back to Paul and his Corinthian friends. I'll take some liberty with his writing. (There is some small comfort in the fact that I'm certainly not the first, and probably not the last, to do so. That makes me, at least, not bad.)

I suggest that Paul's weak-strong statement ("when I am weak, I am strong") can also be read "When I am bad, then I am good." So, back to double think, huh? Admittedly Paul didn't say that, but he came close to it when he wrote to the Romans: "What shall we say then? Are we to continue in sin that grace may abound?" (Romans 6:1).

Paul's answer: "No way!"

The point is: goodness, like strength, is not self-generated. And doing good things to overcome guilt, that inner insistence that we are not good, is an endless treadmill. We always get off exactly where we started, or may be even a little behind.

Self-generated goodness has a distinct odor to it; you can always sniff it out. It is phony, unreal; it is play-acting. Many people are turned off to that sort of ungood goodness. It is the measure of the hypocrite, and who wants that for a model?

Goodness perhaps begins with confession. Confessing weakness, for Paul, opened the door to the possibility of strength. Could it be that confessing that we are not good can open the possibility of our becoming, at least, not bad?

Confessing can get to be a religious habit, and it can tend toward the Pharisee's idea of making a batch of goodness out of a piety recipe. But it *can* be real. It can be a genuine self-encounter, a courageous and honest look at one's heart and soul.

So, if being the somebody that I want to be has to do with being good, just, honest, "OK" (however it may be tagged), where do I go from the confession that I have not yet arrived? What do I do to achieve the goodness, the "OKness," I want in my life?

We are surely not talking about a series of goody acts by which to grab hold of the trophy of goodness. Huckstering a schedule of goodness exercises would probably turn most of us off as tight as a tap with a new washer. The end of such a quick and easy purchase of goodness is bound to be phony, and the end of that is another round of self-rejection and condemnation for being suckered into buying cheap goodness.

Most probably we are not in search of a formula for sainthood. We can be good, OK, without halos. It seems that we are seeking a simple, modest goodness which would get lost with the advertising of it. We don't want to be Mr./Mrs./Ms. Supergood, fending off temptations like repelling insects with bug spray, doing the fantastic and applaudable good deeds, being singled out as a stellar and singular example of "what it means to be good."

We may not seek headlines for our goodness, but it feels good to get clapped on the back and told, "Hey, that was pretty neat, what you did. By me, you're OK." In some ways we are looking for confidence that we are on the right track, some feeling that the track is heading in the right direction, some indication that we are not standing still on the track, but have some movement (at whatever speed).

What follows, then, is not a schedule of exercises for moral muscle building; it is not a foolproof plan for converting oneself into a saint. It is a broad outline for those who want a simple goodness, a confidence about getting there, and yet some assurance that it is never really finished, done, perfected.

It has to do with wants. So very much begins with what we want. Whatever we deeply want, we deeply care about. Not wanting is not caring. And not caring is the sort of anti-hope that shunts us off into despair. Jesus' concern with sin was not so much what folk did, as what they did not do. The religious officials were the ones who did NOT help the man who was mugged and left on the side of the road. It was the prodigal's brother who would NOT accept him back into the family. It was the forgiven servant who would NOT forgive his colleague. They despaired that any positive action made any difference, that every thing is, in the words of Ecclesiastes, "useless." If it doesn't matter, if it can't make any difference, why do anything?

It is the wanting, at its deepest level, that is our motivating force to care enough to let life matter. If we can learn to want and learn what our wants are all about, then life matters enough to care, and the first caring that moves toward being a decent somebody is to care about oneself.

The American colonialists had the right idea. Their flag warned, "Don't tread on me." There is a profound sense of self-respect in that warning. It is to say: I am no doormat, no plush carpet to absorb the shock of someone's rude tromping. "Don't tread on me" is a warning, but it is also a statement of self-respect.

Martin Luther King, Jr., led a movement for self-respect. Refusing to sit in the back of the buses, not accepting a for-whites-only society, the civil rights movement was the catalyst that brought a new sense of self-respect to millions. Goodness was redefined. Before learning to care about themselves, Blacks were told they were "good n_____ers" if they had a bowing and scraping respect for white folks, but complete self-forgetfulness for themselves. But they learned to want something more than this intolerably restricted existence. They took the full measure of themselves and found they were just as human, as intelligent, as capable, as good as any one else. Suddenly "good n_____erism" was exposed for the raw evil it is, and black people began to want. They wanted equal jobs, opportunities, education, justice. They wanted a life, not confined to places for "Colored Only." Now that their self-respect had uncovered their long-repressed wants, suddenly, as early morning fog is burned away to let the sun in, their lives mattered, and they longed for new and meaningful experiences.

On a recent radio program, Betty Friedan spoke about being back in the kitchen and enjoying it. But it was different, being back in the kitchen this time. Now it was for fun, a kind of dabbling in gourmet cooking. She was back in the kitchen because she wanted to be there, not because society had declared that the kitchen was her place in life, that if she was to be acceptable as a woman, she was to serve her man by hustling up his victuals, being what they used to call a "good" woman. For Betty and for a lot of other women, "being a good woman" was not a laurel to be bestowed on them by accepting a kitchen role in life (or that of a sex-cat, or that of a docile, admiring female). Being a good woman began with respect, not gained in the kitchen, but within the private recesses of one's own being, with some pledge of loyalty of oneself as a *bona fide* person. It was to care about oneself, according to one's wants, not according to the role expectations society has long laid upon women.

For so long, it has been grilled into us in church and home that goodness begins with **J**esus first, **O**thers second, and **Y**ourself last. And, of course, that all spells JOY. It also spells self-rejection. It did spell what I have refused to spell, "good n_____erism." But it most certainly never did spell joy.

This little acrostic was cute, and perhaps it did teach something about a sense of loyalty to Jesus. But it completely overlooked a sense of Jesus' loyalty to persons, of his sense of respect for persons, even when they had lost their own respect. More to the point is Jesus' quotation of Leviticus 19:8, "Love your neighbor as yourself." That is to say, love of neighbor begins with self-love, with respect, with caring for oneself. If we are to love others as we love ourselves, and if we have little regard for self, then our love for others will be of little consequence.

Now comes assertiveness. There are training groups in almost every city ready to take your bucks and teach you how to care enough about yourself to stand up for the self you learn to respect. If it all comes off, the bucks will have been well spent and perhaps the price will have been a bargain.

Assertiveness may begin with learning to say, "No." Only if one cares little enough about self can that person be a pushover, an easy touch. The "No" type of assertiveness is to care about the turf that one needs to be a person, the territorial imperative. It is to say "No" to encroachment. It is to know how to keep poachers off and to keep them from dumping their things on you at their price.

Assertiveness is to realize that what you need, what you must do, what you ought to think is your responsibility and your choice. There is no way to surrender that right without giving up an important piece of yourself, without denying that you matter.

If we want to be good, goodness must begin not only at home, but also closer even, with self.

The process then proceeds to letting someone else matter, to caring about another—to wit: "Love thy neighbor."

Tillich felt that the old Latin word *concupiscientia* had a much wider meaning than lustful relationships. It was not only sexual use of another, with little or no regard for the other person, but it was also making tools of others to gain one's own ends.[7] (It is significant that the ends usually gained by using others are not personal, but have to do with things. The end may be power over others, but the power is not an end in itself and usually gets used to obtain a thing. All this concern with "stuff" is perhaps evidence that the personal dimension is lacking in the self of a thing-centered person. Meaning for such a person would not be self-respect, but "thing respect." We see some of this "thing respect" in the priorities that would put property rights above civil rights.)

Vacations make strange personal combinations, like politics. On one vacation I was introduced to a "fellow-American" (we were in Canada at the time). This "fellow" soon got to a discussion of gun laws. He felt there was a devious plot and that it was to disarm the American public. The harangue went on for about forty-five minutes. At the end of the tirade, he informed me that he was sleeping with two rifles by his bed. I had a ridiculous fantasy. He had slept with his guns for years, thinking that he was gallantly protecting his castle and everything in it. But no one ever came. No siege was laid. No one wanted what he had. He was left alone in bed with his guns, while all the rest of the world was having fun and finding more personable beings with whom to share their beds.

To use and abuse in order to have and hold is to miss both the having and the holding that happens by investing our caring in persons, instead of stuff and the guns to guard it.

If a sense of the good happens to us, then, it really needs to be a by-product. If I am loved in order to gain Brownie points for someone who's more interested in being tagged "good" than that one is in persons, then I get the message, loud and clear, that I'm being used. That's not the kind of love I want; it better not be the sort of love I have for my "neighbors."

We are dealing with a gut-love, a caring that is deep into the inwards. It is love with *pathos,* with feeling, with agony, with craziness, with hilarity, with soberness, and with generosity.

Finally, for the Christian and the Jew, wanting to be "good," acceptable, OK, however it might be expressed, has always been related to loving God. Admittedly, we have the whole thing in reverse order. It ought to be: Love God, love neighbor, love self, but the point of beginning is self, for it is with the self that one loves.

There is a hymn for which I learned to have deep feeling. It has to do with the motivation for loving God. It is ascribed to the great Catholic missionary, Francis Xavier.

> My God, I love Thee; not because I hope for heaven thereby,
> Nor yet because who love Thee not must die eternally.
> E'en so I love Thee and will love, And in Thy praise will sing;
> Solely because Thou art my God, And my Eternal King.
>
> —"My God, I Love Thee"

Maybe that sort of motivation for loving (God or persons) belongs only to the capabilities of saints like Francis Xavier. We can talk (as I have) of the self-giving love that is not simply putting dimes in a machine to get pop. Loving God in order to manipulate him is to misunderstand God. So is the hope of genuinely loving God left only to those who are the super-sacred among us? To those we have called saints?

This is not a put-down for those whose adoration of God ends in some ecstatic experience of him. But it is to ask, for us lesser-lights in the worshiping universe, can we, too, love God with something that approaches this self-giving love, this mystic adoration?

In the Judeo-Christian traditions, loving God always turns back to caring about his creation. It is to have loving care of his world, as stewards. It is a far cry from the idolatry that sees God in the stuff of creation. It is, rather, the acknowledgment of God as Creator who saw his creation as "good." It is to accept God's handiwork as "good" and to cherish it. It is to have loving care of creation.

To be deeply moved by the beauty and the strength of it all, to be captured by an uncontrollable awe of the vastness of the whole, to fall incurably in love with creation is right, is good. It is to love God.

On the sixth day he created persons, and God saw everything that he had made, and behold, it was very good (see Genesis 1:31). We are good. We are capable of even greater good. That all depends upon whether or not we want that greater good.

3. *We want to be wise/important.* To love freely, responsibly, completely, takes wisdom. There is a sort of green, immature love. Its heart is in the right place; it is heading in the right direction; but the heart alone is impatient. Bungling attempts at loving and caring make for embarrassing failures.

Johnny, who's not quite mature, but ripening fast, has fixed his affections on Karen. He's not sure what to do with this onrush of strange feelings. His greenness has made his story the setting for humorists in all generations. He is too bashful, too forward, inappropriate; he fumbles for words. And, perhaps, for the sake of this uncontrollable passion he suffers the most horrible indignity: Karen gets tickled and has no more control of her laughter than Johnny does for his passion. The result: one slightly damaged ego (which aches as if it were irreparably damaged).

Learning to love comes from loving, from taking apart one's failures, from observing, but chiefly by taking Johnny's commendable risk. The sum total of what accrues in all this is wisdom, know-how, or that grand old virtue, common sense.

Whether it is how to make love to Karen, how to catch catfish below the dam, or the savvy it takes to "make it" (whatever that expression may mean to one), wise is an important part of what we want to be. It gives us importance, significance, recognition. Like strength and goodness, it comes in two models: real and phony. And the difference between those two is largely one of effort. Shortcuts result in a veneer of smart. It is work and precision, acting and reflecting, researching and sharing, that make up the hard work that leads to the making of wisdom.

Something inside agrees with the writer of Proverbs:

> Yes, if you cry for insight
>   and raise your voice for understanding,
> if you seek it like silver
>   and search for it as for hidden treasures;
> then you will understand the fear of the Lord
>   and find the knowledge of God.
>
> —Proverbs 2:3-5

He's right; we are begging, pleading, looking for wisdom (however we may interpret it—skill on a job, being the resident computer, having savvy, possessing the sophistication of a philosopher, knowing how to make love to Karen).

How *do* we define wisdom?

Pinpointing with some precision what wisdom is all about might be a technical exercise for a philosopher. It might be a biblical exegete dealing with wisdom literature in learned, but obscure, ways. For our purposes here, let's understand wisdom (however inadequately) as awareness, learning ability, skill (the how-to-sort), and capacity.

Awareness is to be fully awake, with all one's senses in tune to environment. Obviously, there is always more there than can be experienced at any one time. One can't see and be aware of everything around—every individual leaf, every kid running after a kite, every newspaper in every driveway, every plane overhead. Sounds go unheard, feelings unfelt, smells unsmelled. We choose, select whatever we want to focus our senses upon. It is another of our choices, our freedom.

That choice is largely determined by one's awareness of self, of what one wants. To be aware in this way is to know, to become familiar with one's feelings, to recognize them as old friends.

Awareness also has to do with recognizing the feelings of others, without having to lay on them one's own set of sensations. We become aware of persons only as we receive, accurately interpret, and share what our sensors pick up. The subtle but tremendously important nuances between them and us need to be recognized. That sort of sensitive awareness moves us toward wisdom.

Wisdom has to do with learning. Perhaps it may be argued that learning is the process that produces wisdom. If wisdom were only the storing of facts and experiences, maybe learning would only be the process for collecting data. But learning involves choice, decision, will, determination. Learning is not by accident. Of course, accidents teach. Fall flat on the face in the icy street, and one might learn what went wrong and ultimately learn how to walk on ice and stay upright. But it is necessary to choose to learn, to make the event produce the wisdom it has within it. The decison to learn is based on some awareness of the event, its meaning, its possibilities, etc. Then the very process of learning becomes wisdom in action.

Wisdom is also knowing "how to." It is the developing of skills and abilities. It is a source for ego nourishment; it all has to do with adequacy. It is knowing how to swing a golf club, how to decorate a cake, how to make a living, and, of course, how to make love to Karen (Katie, Katherine, Karl, Kyle, whomever). It is the stuff that is stored from the learning bit. It is training muscles and eyes; it is recalling facts and figures; it is diagnosing and responding; it is solving and repairing.

Wisdom is also capacity. It is not only deciding and learning and storing, but it also has to do with how much. No tape measure can surround it; no scales weigh it. Yet wisdom, like stamp collecting, depends on value and volume (and to some degree, on variety).

It is not simply what one knows that makes one wise. In the last few years we seem to have spawned great schools of trivia, facts that relate to nearly nothing. That sort of collecting is something short of wisdom, however impressive its collection might be. Wisdom has to do with living; it is usable, and its usableness determines its value.

There is value in this matter of wisdom. One is wise because he or she knows a lot. Wealth of experiences directly relates to the measure of wisdom. It is the mass, the volume of knowing, that makes one wise. And for all of this I come down on the biblical side of it all where wisdom is that amassing of experiences which requires time. But the piling up of time, of days and years, and the collecting of wisdom are not the same. Many years might have done no more than shore up the prejudices that protect us so well from learning, growing, changing; they are the bulwark against wisdom.

Withall, it seems ripe at this point to recall Santayana.

> It is not wisdom to be only wise,
> And on the inward vision close the eyes,
> But it is wisdom to believe the heart.[8]

Whenever I came home with a bad report card (not a terribly unusual occurrence), my father used to ask me, "Don't you want to *be* somebody?" That is still a rather loaded question. It may need asking now as much as it did then. "Don't you want to *be* somebody?" When Dad asked that question, there was always the unmistakable feeling that if my answer was "yes," then it really was possible to *be* somebody. First, I needed to determine that I *wanted* to be somebody.

What Do You Want?

There was a knock at my apartment door. The first flash of reaction was one of annoyance. It was one of those rare at-home-alone times, and I was deeply settled into a Mozart symphony and a book. But it was late, very late, about one in the morning. By the time I had gotten to the door, my fears met me there with a lot of grim possibilities.

No one was visible through the peephole, but while I was trying to search for some recognizable form on the other side of the door, I was startled by a second knock.

"Yes? Who's there?"

There was some inaudible mumble on the dark side of the door.

Drunk! The angers now outnumbered the fears. There was a sour tone to my voice, "What do you want?"

Then a woman's voice, close to the opening edge of the door: "I guess that's my trouble."

"What?"

"I don't know what I want. I really don't."

I opened the door. She was leaning against the doorpost. She looked frightened and puzzled. She kept on leaning and looking at her patent-leather shoes. She shook her head.

"You really got to the meat of it. What *do* I want?" She turned to look at me and sized me up while she was still talking. "Now, if I knew that, I'd know right where to begin. I mean, where to get started, what to spend all this stuff called life for."

An unknown, female philosopher at my door at one in the morning, complaining about not knowing what she wanted! At this point I wasn't sure what I wanted, either. I wasn't in the mood for philosophizing about her "want" dilemma; I knew that much.

I did not want her, at least, not particularly.

What I thought I wanted was interrupted by a somewhat dumpy woman, thirtyish, I would judge, who, for whatever reason (God only knows) knocked on my door to tell me she didn't know what she wanted.

She pushed away from the doorpost, looked smack inside me with a questioning pair of green eyes, and asked, "Do you know what you want?"

"Well, I, uh, I suppose I don't exactly—What do you mean?"

She hunched her shoulders, lifted her arms like tree limbs, and gave me a half smile. I took the gesture to mean "welcome to the don't-know-what-you-want club." Then she turned and walked down the hall to the elevator. It was as if she had just sunk a dry well at my door. She only had to wait a few seconds. I stood at the door, transfixed by puzzlement. Just before she got into the elevator, she sent me that same shrugging gesture, then walked in, and went down. I have not seen the plump lady with the green eyes since.

4 Why Can't Somebody Tell Me What I Want?

Today I filled out a proxy. The annual meeting of my insurance company is about to happen. As one of their insurance protectees, I am invited to attend, have my say, and vote my wishes. Since I don't want to attend, have nothing particular to say, I won't be there to vote my wishes. So I have appointed a man whom I have never met to vote my wishes for me. It's all legal, they tell me, and it is done to facilitate the operation of the company. OK. So long as they don't raise my premiums and keep paying my claims promptly, they can appoint J. Heskamp Burpington (or whomever) to vote my wishes for me.

Proxy voting is a fine idea. I don't have to spend time finding out what the insurance issues are these days. Decisions are made, and if there is risk involved, I am happily ignorant of it. If the decisions are bummers and prove embarrassing, that's Burpington's concern.

Why can't there be life proxies? They just might work wonders, and some enterprising somebody could make a bundle in the process. "Not sure what you want to be? Send five dollars to Dr. I. D. Sidum, and your decision will come to you by return mail." If that plump woman with the green eyes had only knocked at the door of some person like Dr. Sidum, the whole course of her life might have been different.

Of course, the truth is (to put it in innovative truisms), no one can spit for me, make love for me, or decide my wants for me. That's all mine. There is help, advice, and there are techniques (don't do it against the wind, etc.), but the doing is my own. If I try to proxy that away, I would be denying a large part of that reality that is me.

Maybe folks, like the plump woman with the green eyes, are scared of really getting into their wants. It can have an anxious edge to it. It can feel as if one is prying open a Pandora's box. All those wants would be let loose where I can see them, recognize them, feel them, smell them—what a frightening fantasy! I just might be at the mercy of the whole lot of them, enticing me to think about all those wild things, luring me to do weird acts, tempting me to enjoy stuff that I have successfully resisted all my life. No wonder it seems scary; it is!

But, perhaps there is something else in that box we assume to be Pandora's. (Her name, by the way, means "all the gifts.") In that box, locked up so tightly, we may find excitement, promise, and that strange, nebulous thing called fulfillment. It's all in the same box: wishes that destroy and wishes that put it all together; wants that ruin and wants that really make it; dreams that are vicious and dreams that are full of love and intimacy. One box!

Where shall we find the courage to pry it open and begin to peer inside to find out what's there?

If faith has to do with the living out of our lives with some sense of promise, but without perfect assurance, if it has to do with the reality of risk and excitement of accomplishment, then faith might be a source for such box-opening courage. It might feel like this: sure, in the box are all kinds of mind-eating, life-cheating bugbears, but by the grace of the Lord God, I can handle that. I am not going to be overwhelmed by my own desires. It would, after all, be no act of faith to sacrifice all (or even most) of my wants on the altar of the idol, Fear.

(Now, I am beginning to feel some anger boiling. The object is not yet clear, but it is whoever, whatever has made me keep the lid tight on the box of my wants, my desires, my passions. By God! They are mine, and I will do with them just what I want. What is this that would deny me that intensely personal right to know my own wants? What prison keeper would lock me away from the source of my own fulfillment? I see it more plainly now. It is not the wants and passions that are locked in a box. I am in the box, and I want out. Right now!)

To live by faith means to declare one's independence. It is to be free from being told what to want. It is to refuse to be manipulated by the slick-paged and slicker-tongued advertisers who would readily be my want-proxies, vote my wishes for me. How very stupid and inept they all must consider me! They must decide what is the right tone and flavor for my life, define for me what is the good life. Having proxied the good for me, then they would proceed to fill it up for me like some hired decorator who knows, far better than I, what goes with what. Whatever that sort of nondeciding is, it isn't faith. "Trust me. You'll simply love it when I'm finished." Balderdash! (and points west!)

OK, I admit that it is not only scary, but hard work, finding out what one really wants, how one wants to live, what fulfillment means to oneself. It's easier to sit with a mug of beer and watch the colored tube flicker and be told what to want.

Like a sinner who had just found salvation, Bud told me, with wide-eyed enthusiasm, how he had discovered that what he had really wanted was an intimate, caring, and sharing relationship. He was right smack in the middle of the good life, he had kept telling himself. At the end of the day, on his prestige job, he came home to his big house in the affluent neighborhood, kicked off his shoes and gave himself, with determined devotion, to the tube. The routine was varied with golf with some buddies who were also "making it." Maggie was there for keeping the whole home operation going (just as Wembly kept the new accounts in running order, back at "the firm"). Something was lacking, and at forty-eight, Bud thought of an affair, but he knew he was too awkward to pull it off. The appetite was there, though, but Bud couldn't get at it. There was a lot more stuff to be had—bigger houses, more expensive cars, all that. But it didn't feel quite right.

Then it hit. It was on the ninth hole, luckily right at the clubhouse. Heart attack!

There were days in the intensive care unit with tubes, monitors, and a television screen that looked like a sales chart. "A real up and down company, that outfit," he thought to himself and chuckled at his own joke. "Up and down, that's what it's all about. I'd rather be up than down. This is down; this is really down! I'd rather be up than.... What would I rather? What do I want?"

Except for all the clinical types, whose humanity peeked through every so often, Bud only saw Maggie. It was just for ten minutes, four times a day. It was almost as if by prescription. The ten minutes quickly became the most important minutes in the whole day. Bud lived for those every-six-hours visits. More was said in those ten-minute slots than they had shared in all their eighteen years together. He watched Maggie leave after one visit; she stopped and turned at the corner of the nurses' station and waved. "My God, that's it! That's what I want, more than anything else in my life—Maggie! She's the most important thing in my whole life!"

Bud was out of the hospital earlier than expected, but not earlier than Maggie had expected.

"I know now," he told me. "It's people, and Maggie's at the top of the list." He blew into her ear; she snuggled up close to him. "You know, Pastor, there ought to be a better and less expensive way of finding out what you want than heart attacks!"

It was to be the first of a long repetition of times that I was to hear Bud claim that he didn't resent his heart attack. He found what he wanted, what he was living for. In fact, it was only the beginning of Bud's discovery of his wants, but they were *his* now, not those that someone in Bud's position *ought* to want.

The church could be less risky than a heart attack, far less costly, if it assumed that, in the practice of its faith, enabling people to get at their wants was a vital part of its mission. More often than not (at least, not seldom) churches assume the right to proclaim what people ought to want, indeed what they will want, if they are to be reckoned as good.

There's some sadness to Dean Kelley's book on church growth. In it, he claims that the growing churches are those who lay on people what they ought to be wanting.[1] If they want what the church wants them to want, they will then be counted among the good. And who wants to be among the bad?

But the church cannot determine whether I am good or bad, and it does not really know what I want, or even what I ought to want. It could help me find out. It could be supportive of my search. It could care where I was in my inquiry. It could affirm my desire to do the looking in the first place. All of which would go a long way in generating a faith in me for myself and trust of my wants. It would help me believe more in people, in my environment, and in the purposes of the Lord God, who is in the process of fashioning all this so that love comes out on top of it all, in the end.

My word to the church is: don't tell me what I ought to want; do tell me what it is OK to want. Don't tell me what to believe; do tell me that belief, trust, faith are possible. Don't give me iron-hasped boxes for my wants; do help me get my box open. Don't ask for my proxy; do affirm my suspicion that I *can* act on my own wishes—and thus move toward the fulfillment the church often proclaims.

Sam Keen has some directions about getting serious on the business of wanting and assuming responsibility for one's wanting. Keen offers a way to get at it. But, first, let's put Sam Keen in context: In an interview, he was concerned about a sort of bi-polar existence. It had to do, on the one hand, with "grounding," and on the other, with "soaring." Grounding has to do with the reality of one's life. It is one's life story; it is one's myths; it is one's encounters. Soaring is ecstasy; it is transcendence; it is (in its best sense) spiritual, unlimited, free.

Keen goes on to connect soaring with wanting:

> Soaring appears to be rooted in the capacity to desire, a capacity which is crippled in many people—not because of what has happened in the past, but because of what did *not* happen. Our "wanting" is our motivation to act, and if your desiring is not consummated in act, over and over, it diminishes or is lost.[2]

There is a process to soaring, as Keen sees it, and it begins with imaging, stretching the imagination, stargazing. Imaging is dreaming, visualizing. It is to allow oneself to be seduced by "what-if?" The second movement in the process has to do with wishing. It is to begin to feel the good of the imaging, to project oneself into the middle of its fulfillment. Then there is wanting. Wanting is determining to get the thing one has imaged; a more nonsoaring term might be "goal setting." Wanting then becomes willing, determining a course of action; it is getting down to the tactics of how it is to be realized. It is plotting out achievement. Finally, there is action, and without action, the whole process is aborted. And when action doesn't happen, Keen contends, the interest level dies, and it becomes much easier to keep the lid on the box of wants. In fact, at such time as that, you don't need an iron hasp. The lid lies flat of its own weight . Use it, or lose it!

But, suppose that you decide to use it, to take the gamble. The lid begins to come off; the wants begin to be seen and recognized. You are overwhelmed, not because they are monsters, but because there are so many, and at every possible level. Wants about having, wants about doing, wants about being, wants about going, wants about becoming. Red wants and green wants, fat wants and skinny ones, sweet wants and some salty ones, quiet wants and wants that are loud and hilarious. There are wants of every shape and kind and color, every smell and flavor. What in the name of Holy Hannah can be done with all these cut-loose wishes, these desires buzzing around in your head? It's choosing time, roll-up-the-sleeves time, hard work time. *Prioritizing* is the going word for it.

Make all those wants get in line—the most important first, then all the rest, in order of rank. They are all a rebellious lot, and they will all scramble to be first in line. The decision is yours; you rank them. However they get ranked, there is one clear understanding to be had: You are the commander-in-chief. Promotions are yours to make; commands are yours; rewards are yours; demotions, discipline, evaluations—it's your command.

Prioritizing gets done by valuing. The process of sorting out values begins to make some order out of the want chaos. Developments by Raths, Simon, Howe, and Kirschenbaum suggest that such a process might look like this: choosing, prizing, and acting.[3]

Choosing means that you do the picking. No proxies can do the deciding. Choosing is to make a choice, based on what suits you, fits your feelings, meets your criteria for beauty, fulfills your dream. It is at this crucial point that one's faith needs to assert, firmly, that choosing on such a basis is good, moral, OK, even commendable.

If choosing is to have meaning, then it needs to come from among other alternatives. If there is only one choice, what choice is that? The once-a-year-you-can't-miss-it sale is on. You are late getting there. There is only one suit in your size left. This one or nothing. Buy it or forget it. Choosing from a number of alternatives means you have other options. When the options are many, there is some room to exercise one's own personality.

Choosing also needs to be at a time chosen by you. When you are put in a bind and made to choose ("I'm sorry, the store closes in five minutes"), another dimension of your freedom is lost.

There needs to be some projection, future-guessing about the what-if nature of choosing. What will the consequences most likely be? Obviously, that sort of guessing needs to develop an edge of accuracy. If the choices are yours, so are the consequences.

Next comes prizing. The choice is made; it needs now to be cradled, protected, cared for, cherished. It needs to feel right, good, acceptable, but more—it needs to be esteemed. Choices made, not because they had to be made, but because you wanted to make them, take on a precious feeling, to wit, value.

Then, as Sam Keen suggested, action is the next step. Stick out the neck, turtle, and move! Action is a kind of moment of creation. It is calling into reality what one has chosen and prized. It is to bring into being what did not exist. It is to give birth, to play the mother part. It is to experience some bone-deep satisfaction, knowing you can make it happen.

So what makes us take the step that ends in action? How does motivation happen? Harry Levinson has written a great book on motivation; he called it *The Great Jackass Fallacy.* The fallacy is an unmistakable one; it is to believe that motivation happens only in two ways: (1) by the whip behind, or (2) the carrot in front. The picture of the whip and carrot is completed by the image of what's in between—the jackass. He is not known for his self-starting motivation. He is apt to be stubborn, and he knows all about resistance. Levinson contends that motivation comes, not by threats and rewards; it comes rather by knowing what one wants, genuinely and deeply wants.[4] And thus we have come back, full circle. The source of our motivation is our wanting.

It all boils down to taking charge of your own living, picking up your own marbles.

It's your life, Bunky.

Don't give it away to another's proxy.

Don't wait for Godot, or anyone else.

Interlude:
To Celebrate Joy

Are You Happy?

"Jim! Jim!"

It was 3:04 A.M., and only a faint light was piercing Jim's deliciously unconscious state.

"Huh? Wha . . .?"

"Jim, are you happy?"

"Hmmmm, unh, probably the furnace, Margaret. Heat. Expanding pipes. Little noisy. It's nothing, Dear. Go back to sleep."

Jim rolled over and punched his pillow, gave himself a settling-down wriggle.

"No, Jim. I didn't say anything about noise. I asked, 'Are you happy?' "

Jim did a slow turn toward Margaret. "It could be that pizza. Take a couple of Alka-Seltzers."

"James! James! Happy! Are you happy?"

His first clear awareness was that whatever Margaret had in mind had to be dealt with before further sleep. Jim drew a deep breath, as if he were trying to inhale patience from somewhere.

"Margaret, what is it?"

"Are you happy?"

"What happy? You want happy at 3:00 A.M.? Not now, Margaret, we'll make love tonight. Right now, happy is sleep. OK?"

Jim flipped over, pulled the blanket around his neck. It was a final gesture; it meant "Don't bother me!"

Margaret turned over the other way. They were now back to back. She watched the shadow of a leaf flicker in the moonlight on the floor. Jim had gone back to sleep.

Time Out for Joy

You have been reading, and I have been writing. Let's declare a time out, an old-fashioned recess. "Interlude" sounds right. "Break" feels familiar.

There needs to be some time in a book about wanting that makes wanting seem possible. Left out in the never-never horizon of "when my ship comes in" makes wanting seem unreal. Sometimes wants happen, become reality. It is that reality that I am proposing that we share.

It will be built around calling up a memory; it will be letting that relived memory bring a fresh experience of promise. It happened once; it can happen again, differently, to be sure. But joy can strike again, and in the same place.

So here's an interlude for remembering an experience of joy. Let the memory of it float around long enough to allow you to recall as much detail as possible and to savor the whole experience again—the taste of it, the smell of it, the look of it, the sounds of it, and most of all, the feel of it.

Get caught up in it again, and let it bring its own sense of refreshing and renewal. Let the joy recalled wash over you like a cool shower in hot July. There is something sparkling about it that both cleanses and restores. Invigorating. Energizing. Inspiring.

Let your memory tickle promise awake. How long has it been since you really anticipated something, looked forward to it with that sort of impatience of a kid, two days before a birthday? Excitement, that's where we're headed—getting caught up in the reliving of a memory of joy that didn't die with yesterday. It's above time's tenses. It is then, now, whenever.

Let it, this memory, enliven you in places that are dormant, dulled, grown insensitive. Let it tighten some strings and twang a little ditty inside you. The old hymn had the idea:

> Down in the human heart,
> Crushed by the tempter,
> Feelings lie buried that grace can restore;
> Touched by a loving heart,
> Wakened by kindness,
> Chords that are broken will vibrate once more.
> —Fanny Crosby, "Rescue the Perishing"

Such a loving heart, among others, can be your own. After all, loving starts with learning to care about oneself, doesn't it?

Let's get started. Pick a memory of a time of joy. Make it as current as possible. Last week is great; yesterday is better. Six years ago is still real. Don't push for it; let it come as naturally as it can. Now, put this book down and let a memory of joy happen. Don't think hard, as if you were trying to recall a right answer for a test. Just let it bubble up. Put the book down now. . . .

Got it?

O.K. Let's get into it. What other people were in the experience with you? What did they mean to you? How did they happen to be a part of your joy? What did they contribute? Did they know you were having a rare and great experience? How did you share it with them? With others later? Is there someone you could share it with now, who could really reexperience it with you?

Where did it all happen? What did the environment feel like? What do you remember about the scenery? What was the weather like? Can you remember (this may call for some stretching) what you were feeling just before the event? What really triggered it for you?

Go back and relive it all again. Recreate the whole scene—the colors, the sounds, the feelings. Sit back, comfortably; close your eyes; put on a record and tell your mind, "Play it again, Sam" (or whatever you call your mind). Close your eyes now . . .

Joy is real. It can happen again. As I relived my experience, I was struck by the element of spontaneity to it all. I didn't make it happen. I didn't manufacture it. I don't think I could have predicted it. But I was there; *it* didn't simply spontaneously appear. I made the effort to be there. There was some risk involved. I did some things I don't usually do. I knew that the others there might not understand or appreciate my out-of-the-ordinary actions. But I wanted to do it anyway, and their warm reaction was a solid part of the experience of joy.

Let's see if we can get some handles on this elusive thing called joy. The handles just might give some lift to our wanting. I suspect, however, that we shall not be able to do a postmortem on our experience in order to put a sliver of it under a microscope to observe its cell structure. We might follow a rose lover's advice: "Don't pick off the petals to enjoy the rose. Maybe don't even pick the rose."

We can at least look at joy and reflect on how it seems to be put together.

Joy has variety to it. It is not just country ham and black-eyed peas. It is steak and wine; it is sweet-and-sour pork; it is turkey and dressing; it is rice and curried lamb.

Joy is hilarity, and that sort of joy is just about always shared. It is sharing a belly-shaking joke with a friend. It is that sort of story in which the laughter spills out before you can tell the punch line. Hilarity is a joyous sense of abandon. It is rowdy and boisterous. It builds itself up to a fever pitch, and it wears you out and leaves you to a sweet sense of fatigue.

The prototype is King Henry VIII and his court—loud and bawdy, lusty and lively. It's offensive to quiet types, and it may get out of hand and take on a destructive aspect. Sometimes we pay great prices for it to happen. We go to sporting events to scream and yell and experience hilarity. We buy our passes, at the rate of a high-priced meal, at six flags over whatever, in order to be driven recklessly up and down steel hills, in order to be flung into dizziness by mechanical contraptions, in order to gorge ourselves on quick food fare. Sometimes we have a ball, a real wow-inspiring time. Then again, it doesn't quite happen. "It was just too hot!" "Well, if we hadn't had Cynthia along." "It was the long lines." Whatever.

But hilarity is possible, and it is a kind of joy. It doesn't make sense to hide from it; it makes less sense to be afraid of it.

Ecstasy is close to hilarity, but it is not quite the same. The dictionary makes it close kin to rapture, extreme delight, being carried away, and Roget says it is like "rapture, joy, transport, bliss, exaltation; gladness, intoxication, enthusiasm; trance, frenzy, inspiration." It is to be drunk without booze, to be on a drugless high. It is some unseen angel of joy that takes control of mind, body, and soul and sends joy pulsating through the whole being. We quiver and quake and are vaguely aware that we're really not in control just then. But something inside that opts for abandon reassures us with the whisper, "So, who wants control?"

Probably our most common experience with that sort of ecstasy is orgasm. Part of the tragedy of our time is that sexual ecstasy is seen, on the one hand, as some necessary and very unclean evil, and on the other, as the only *raison d'être,* the whole purpose of life. The truth is obviously somewhere else. I liked Concordia Press's advertisement for its sex education series. In big, bold, red letters on a black background, it proclaimed: "SEX IS GOD'S IDEA!"

What a strange idea to suppose that our Creator would give us all sexual equipment—physical and emotional—then sternly warn us, "But don't you ever use it!" But it is precisely that conclusion that robs us of sexual joy. Surely there is no reason to deny oneself the exquisite pleasure of sex, except to enhance that joy or to gain a greater one.

The other side of the coin is to view sex as the only real aim in life: the only reason for getting out of bed is to get back in again. While one way of denying the pleasure of sex is to restrict it with compulsiveness, the other is to be driven to the experience of it, with obsessiveness. Often is not enough and variety is beyond satisfaction. The sex hunger becomes an insatiable maw. The real Don Juan, stripped of the romantic and dashing facade, is lonely, full of self-doubt, and driven.

Sexual ecstasy is a real joy, a genuine part of human capacity for pleasure. And the Lord God looked at what was created, and said, "Look! That's good!"

Then I think God also said, "Yes, that's good, but that's not all there is."

It may be our most common experience of it, but there is more to ecstasy than sexual pleasures.

Ecstasy is also to be caught up in an experience that can best be described as spiritual. Ecstasy is to be outside one's self, as this untranslated Greek word means. It is to discover another dimension, another reality, another world. Spiritual ecstasy is, for the most part, a strange concept to us practical, commonsense types. It feels unreal. At best, it is imagination; at worst, it is madness. Why is it that those who seek such ecstatic experiences seem to be misfits? Why do we see them as detached from reality? Are they really the spiritual pariahs?

Our faith ought to be strong enough to allow us to ask some "what ifs." What if there is another reality different from that we have grown used to? What if there is a way to experience this "other" reality through meditation, imagery, yoga? What if we were really denying *ourselves*? What if our own faith came from such roots? And what if spiritual ecstasy were a way to experience wholeness?

At this juncture in my life, I can ask the questions better than I can answer them (which has been true at most other junctures, as well). But, I am asking them. I am asking them with head and heart. I am reading and experimenting, listening and experiencing. I have tasted something of this ecstasy; there is something real. It is both frightening and promising. It has the exciting edge of discovery to it, and it is demanding in time and discipline. There is some joy there (there is some sadness, too). I want to know that joy, even at the expense of the sadness.

Ecstasy is a kind of spasm of joy that cannot last forever. It is too intense, and the human structure is not built to spend large hunks of time in it. When its delightful paroxysm is over, there comes the delicious and relaxed afterglow. Afterglow is contentment, and it can be sustained over a period of time. Contentment can follow, but it is not dependent upon the wilder experience of ecstasy.

Paul wrote about contentment to the Philippians. "I have disciplined myself to be content, whatever the situation" (see Philippians 4:11). He was not a man without ambitions (his deep-boned wants are exposed in Romans 10), but he had learned to experience contentment without attaining all his desires. It is a learning, a disciplining. It can be a source of all the joys we can know.

Then, there is WOW!

Joy does not (in spite of Ma Bell's advice) always call ahead. If we are not so tightly defended against a good time, we may just luck into it and know the surprise of it.

One mellow-toned Friday, in the gray middle of winter, I bought a bottle of Catawba wine. I had fantasized a quiet evening by the fire, with Barbara: the kids tucked away in bed; the cork popped on the wine, some sharp cheddar; and the evening would flow from here to there. I came home with my treasure tucked under my arm. "I have a surprise for you," I said. She turned and looked at me, almost laughing. "Boy! Have I got a surprise for you!" she said. What was this to be? Guess who can out-surprise whom? "Someone is coming to see us, and you can just wait and see who it is," she continued. I guessed everyone from Anwar Sadat to J. Percy Pinwinkle. Neither Barbara nor the girls would give me the slightest hint. Time was in their conspiracy and slowed down to a turtle crawl. Finally, a car pulled into the driveway. I ran outside, and out of the car hopped my brother, whom I had not seen in years. The Catawba went in three directions; we talked and laughed and discovered that time had jerked itself into its jet-speed mode. The weekend was gone, and I savored being surprised.

There is a minor-league joy, but a real one, nonetheless. It is relief. It is to come to that sighing end of hurting, worrying, working. It is *aaaaahhhhh!* It is bicarbonate for a stomach on fire. It is the car pulling into the driveway when the kid has been out too late. It is hearing the five-o'clock whistle when you've been stacking lumber all day in the ninety-degree heat. There's some significance to relief; it is somewhere out there, on the periphery of joy.

No potpourri of joys would be complete (and this one makes no aim at getting them all) without achievement. Perhaps there is a flavor of relief to achievement too, but that's a by-product. To have finished the job and done it well, to have poured energy and thought, skill and confidence into a project, to see it take shape and be done—that is achievement; that is joy.

It was a clear, clean May day. We sat puffed up with pride, among other puffy parents, and watched our son receive his degree in architecture. This was his payoff for all those long nights hunched over his slanted desk. Five years of climbing over frustrations, like some gigantic mental and psychological obstacle course. Now was the golden moment, the long line, the dean's hand clasp, the head of the department with the diploma. Achievement! Joy! (I'm sitting there, musing: *We got one through; maybe we can help pull through three more!)*

Self-actualizing is the going word for it in psycho-parlance, the top rung in Abraham Maslow's ladder. It is, perhaps, the joy least known. But, when it becomes the style of our living, when we can shuck off our unneeded dependencies and allow ourselves to be graced by our interdependencies, when we can put into motion all we can do, and when we are growing and developing ourselves, then we are into a joy that is the most sustaining of all. It doesn't dry up unless we do. It doesn't get monotonous and boring unless we let it. It doesn't become fruitless and without meaning unless we allow it.

David Spangler, following Maslow, spells out what the self-actualizing person is like. Reality is seen as it is, rather than as one's deficiency needs demand it to be. The self-actualizer is drawn by the unknown, allured by adventure, seduced by the mysterious. Such a person is not motivated by the need to be accepted (self-acceptance has become a fact of life); motivation comes from the need to grow, learn, develop, evolve. The self-actualizing person is spontaneous and free from the need to conform or the need to be different, working in the widest possible framework, not allowing life to be narrowed mindlessly by tradition or meaninglessly by expectations. The self-actualizing person wants people for themselves, not to fill some deficiencies in his or her life. Relationships are not reduced to: (1) "Tell me I'm OK" or (2) picking "safe" people who won't disturb one's own world view (or more aptly, one's "parochial-view"). Such an actualizer has the uncommon ability to appreciate the little, the delicate, the at-hand, the inexpensive.[1]

Enough. The self-actualizer *knows* the joy of becoming.

Along about here we need to get into ways of experiencing the joys we have been looking at. Window-shopping is cheap but hardly satisfying.

In different times, long past, the witch doctors would read the entrails of chickens to determine whether or not some enterprise had any possibility of success. Modern witch doctors do the same thing with a "feasibility study." Here's our beginning—with chicken or computer—is it feasible for you? Can you experience joy? You have the answer. Only you can total up the pros and cons and know the sum and its meaning. At least, make the cons prove themselves, throw the doubts at them, and insist on solid evidence. Don't misread your chicken; insist upon another opinion.

We can begin by looking at our capacity for anticipation.

Anticipation, literally, means to take possession of beforehand. It is to own one's dreams. It is excitement now for some future event.

It is to plant and nourish; it is to plan and build. It is to lay a claim on one's future.

Anticipation has its own joy; it is the joy of expecting. To have run out of something to look forward to is to have depleted a large supply of living. Maybe the years tend to take away the Night-Before-Christmas thrill, but something of that uncontrollable anticipation needs to spill over into the ages of one's life. Sometimes anticipation is more thrilling than participation. Keats wrote of the situation in his "Ode on a Grecian Urn":

> Bold lover, never, never canst thou kiss,
> Though winning near the goal—yet, do not grieve;
> She cannot fade, though thou has not thy bliss;
> For ever wilt thou love, and she be fair![2]

We studied that poem in school, just before the Christmas recess, and our professor gave us an over-the-holidays assignment: to determine "whether the anticipation of osculation was greater than participation therein." The reports seemed to indicate that, in this case, participation also became anticipation. We were not commissioned to investigate beyond the osculatory stage.

Somewhere along the way, if anticipation is to be saved from fruitless daydreams about ships that never come in, about loves that never happen, anticipation needs to be fulfilled. We need to become more than specators titillated by fantasies, who are satisfied to remain seated for the next show. Anticipation seems to feed on participation, and as we boys reported to our professor, after our Christmas vacation research, participation brings a new and heightened level of anticipation.

What is our potential for participating in joyous happenings? I have had the guilties at one time or another and counted myself out of something genuinely joyous. I would decide to work, making excuses that I had to get some jobs done. I thought about the "sweet" sympathy I would get—"That poor, poor fellow is *so* dedicated to his job." But no sympathy is as sweet as being at the parade, at the party, at the fun time. True, sometimes the job does *have* to be done, but, if in the doing of it we do not buy some greater participation in joy, maybe we need to counsel with our local, friendly employment agency.

What is the height, width, depth; what is the volume of our capacity to participate fully in the joys at hand?

Trust has to do with the experience of joy. If we experience joy, we need to have enough trust to believe that it is OK to be caught by joy. The pious puritan within needs to be set at rest. That puritan needs to investigate the deep distrust of anything that smacks of fun. A little fun might not be bad, the puritan thinks, but only if you earn it, and the earning ought always to outstrip the "funning." Why isn't it the other way around? "No, you absolutely cannot go to work until you have had your fun for the day!" "You must eat your dessert, before you may have your spinach." "Now, don't argue, dear. You must have a round of poker with the guys before you cut the grass."

All of which may be stretching it into wild shapes, but why is fun suspect? Why it is not judged by better standards? Is it that we do not trust ourselves with delight? Do we feel protected by drudgery? Protected against what? Work can destroy us, and it is far more likely to bring on heart attacks, strokes, and mental breakdowns, than play. Maybe work is more the culprit than fun. Now if we can only just get paid for having a jolly good time.

Can we really trust fun, delight, joy? Probably we can trust them far more than most of us do, but there is a destructive kind of pursuit of joy. I use "pursuit" because it never seems to happen; it is always at least one jump down the road. It is the Don Juan pursuit. There is never enough, and one is driven by some insatiable fiend within, for more intensity, more excitement, more often. It is a fractured pursuit of joy that is a mad need to escape from one's self, one's freedom, and one's responsibility. It is as if joy were pursued for its anesthetizing value, and if the pursuit—Don Juan style—doesn't get it, the chemical kind can. And the mind is blown, like a candle—out!

Joy depends on trust, especially where shared joy is concerned, and the unshared kind seems to be incomplete. It seems that the simplest joy is magnified by sharing it. Its dimensions stretch out when someone else is in it with us; the colors are more vivid and intense; the tone is clearer, purer; the whole experience is more immediate.

It is from persons that the whole experience seems to begin. Joy is people born. And that takes some trusting, as well. It is to trust oneself with people. It is to be convinced that "I may not be great, but I'm OK, and that's for sure." The person whom I must learn to trust first, in the experiencing of joy with others, is me. I have no great gifts, no extraordinary ability to entertain. But I can enjoy people, well, some people. I can be a part of their bunch, share belly-laughs, be silly, listen to and tell tales, take and be taken seriously, give and receive, embrace and be embraced. Just about every joy I've known has had somebody's name on it. I want my joy with people.

So, what is joy?

Joy is . . .

Well, joy is simple. It may have a good many intricate variations; basically, it is pure and simple, and it depends far more on attitude and trust than on privilege and money.

Joy is *pro tempore.* From whatever theological camp one comes, one is apt to agree that eternal bliss is not a this-life experience. Joy gets used up, is disposable, and we need to look for other experiences.

Joy is close in time and space. Far-off stuff may be never-never stuff. Joy is at hand. Joy is now.

Joy is to be had.

Up There? In the Sky?

"It's extraordinary!"

"Oh? What's extraordinary?"

"The steeple on the church." His words bristled with that starched accent of a visitor from India. "I did not suppose that your churches would have that sort of symbol on them."

Mrs. Philomeyer was obviously puzzled, in fact, doubly puzzled, but she was determined to understand Mr. Prayatnam's statement. With her innate politeness, she asked, "Would you explain that to me, Mr. Prayatnam? I don't think I quite understand what you're saying. Steeples are quite common, you know, and I assure you we don't really have a very unique one."

"I did not expect to be reminded of a temple of Siva, in America."

"Temple of Siva?"

"Yes, they all have a *lingam* symbol. It is the sign of Siva."

"I'm afraid that you'll have to explain again. *Lingam* must be a Hindi word, and I assure you that your English is much better than my Hindi." Mrs. Philomeyer focused her attention on Mr. Prayatnam, showing the proper interest her etiquette required.

"Well, your closest teacher to the way of Siva, in the Western world, would be Dr. Freud. He called it the phallic symbol."

Mrs. Philomeyer coughed.

"Pardon. I have a slight cold," she lied. "Uh, well, no." Again the cough. Composure was slow in coming back. "No, I think, uh, it is not a, er, *that* at all."

"It is supposed to point to something?"

"Uh, well, yes. It, er, points to our hope, our Christian hope."

"I see. What is your hope, Mrs. Philomeyer, your Christian hope?"

"Our hope is in Jesus Christ."

"Up there? In the sky?"

"He ascended, you know, went up into heaven."

"Oh, yes. I do remember that."

"Perhaps you would like to see our sanctuary?"

"Please." Mr. Prayatnam glanced back at the steeple and scratched his head.

5 Hope 'Way Up in the Sky . . . Somewhere

There is an undeniable malaise about our time. It is a thinly disguised despair. Oh, there is music—they call it—light music even. But behind it all there is a relentless, driving, pounding beat that catches you up and carries you along to some inescapable ending, while the oversized woofers pulsate with low notes that feel dark and foreboding.

"Doonesbury," "The Wizard of Id," and "Andy Capp" are un-comic comics that have lost sight of "funny," as we all seem to have. When will anything good happen to Charlie Brown? Will the Great Pumpkin rise out of the sincere pumpkin patch? Linus's unshakable hope is put down by his sister, and even his girl friend loses her hold on her share in his hope.

There is an underlayer of futility about our times. Television programs seem to have at least one thing in common (with the exception of commercials)—something is going to go wrong, something bad is going to happen, and it usually does. The news substantiates it; comedies set it up so we can laugh at it; dramas play it out for all it is worth. We seem to be hooked on tragedy and disaster.

There's an obsession about impotency—everything from the bedroom variety to the powerlessness of the poor. It is not only that one cannot fight city hall, but also city hall cannot fight its own battles meaningfully now. There is no strident Mayor Daley or Tom Pendergast on the scene anymore. Crooked politicians are grubby little characters, filching the till and playing around with women who sell their bodies for whatever will bring back some comfort to their tense bodies.

Everything from "A" to "Z" and back again has been written about the hopelessness reflected in the drug scene of the young and the booze scene of their elders. In a nutshell, they portray our days without hope—since there is no hope, the uppers and downers enable one simply to cope.

I know a psychiatrist who told his patient, "I don't want to talk about your despair; it's too depressing."

What's the sum total of all this? Can there be any hope? Does it make sense to want, to want anything at all? Something seems to be dying. People? Yes, but people have died before and they always will. Ideals? Morals? Well, they have been comers and goers, as well. Something more profound than all that. Something is dying that we are not merely observing. Something is dying and we are part of it.

William Irwin Thompson, former professor of history at Massachusetts Institute of Technology, has had a feeling for this demise of our time and, using the analogy of a phonograph record, concludes:

> Something has already happened, something so vast that all our social-science descriptions of man cannot add up to it. The record of civilization is over, and like a record at its end, it keeps going on with the noise of a needle stuck in its rut: the revolution of the workers, the protest of the young, the new creations of the avant-garde, the rise of new forms of sexual liberation, the appearance of new religions. This side of history is over, and on the other side is myth.[1]

The meaningless rhythm of a needle at the end of a record's music—*schawhump, schawhump, schawhump.* There are dancers on the floor like crazed marathoners, holding each other up, dazed by fatigue and oblivious to the end of the music. Is this our age, this grand and glorious, this swift and sophisticated era of ours? Some feel that our age is not only dying, but that it is already moribund.

Frederick Ferré, Professor of Philosophy at Dickinson College, says:

> The most important fact about our current historical situation is hard to accept: that our modern world is in its last days (or already largely ended) and that we are—ready or not, like it or not—entering a turbulent period of transition to a very different world of post-modernity.

> This fact, accepted or not, is occasioning deep spiritual distress, unfocused and shallow though it may presently be. Convulsive shifts are occurring deep in the bedrock of our cultural assumptions. Hitherto mainly unquestioned expectations of continuous growth, hitherto mainly unchallenged virtues of technical expertise, hitherto mainly unexamined images of the future as endless variations on the familiar themes of modernity itself—all have come under scrutiny and have been found wanting.[2]

And, in a further chapter: ". . . there are fatal flaws in the modern world which make its ending certain. . . ."[3]

What are these writers claiming? That event, long prophesized by the sandwich-board prophets? "Repent! The End of the World Draws Near!" Are they predicting some dyspeptic mood in the Kremlin (or the Pentagon) that will bring on the ultimate nuclear disaster we have learned to live with and ignore?

None of these. Our age, our thoroughly modern milieu is toppling, like Shakespeare's Sir Toby Belch, by its own rapacity and gluttony.

We are like children losing a parent. We don't know how to handle it. We don't know what it means. We wonder what will happen. Is there any hope? Does it then make sense to let our selves want anything beyond our output and intake needs for the moment?

Dear old Age, "we hardly knew ye." We thought you'd be around, always. We had just never supposed you were mortal, too. We took you for granted, in spite of our over-picking analyses which we have just now learned to put together, only to find you are dying. We are stunned, numbed. We'd cry, but our eyes and our souls are dry. We are not even scared, but we aren't brave, either. We're just dazed. It's a hard sight to look at, not pretty at all. There's nothing in our catalog that gives us a cue for reacting to it. We just hang loose and try to put a tag on what we do feel. Good-bye, Age—Space, Nuclear, Computer—whatever your name really was. I guess we never really found out what age it was, after all. Shalom!

*

*

*

*

What if it were resurrection time? The day of the phoenix? Out of the ashes, and all that? And, if it were (and let's suppose that it is), what sort of hope would make sense?

No more bigger and better. More and more money won't get it. Climbing up over the skinned heads of erstwhile colleagues is no prize. Even on top, it all would turn sour.

What hope do we want? To what do our steeples point, after all?

Maybe they are pointing the way for my balloon. Here it goes, anyway. Let the ropes loose! Shoot me down if you want, if you can, if you must.

The hope toward which I want to go is to believe that creation—the whole cockeyed thing—in spite of its dying ages, is moving toward wholeness, that sense of wholeness which includes peace, respect. Enough for all, rather than plenty for some. Freedom with equal amounts of responsibility. Justice that gives all society the equal scales in fact, and not just in a statute. That elusive quality we have called humanness—awareness, sensitivity, gentleness, humor. What I hope for is the sense that creation, like we individual human parts of it, has a purpose, that the trend is toward the realization of that purpose, that all creation will "self-actualize" into its age of shalom. It has to be a hope so gigantic that all the hurt and agony, the tragedy and sorrow, the loneliness and hostility, the barbarism and atrocity will have been worth it.

Admittedly, that's some hope!

It's too much to describe. The picture of it is out of focus—hazy like a Hollywood out-of-focus love scene. My vocabulary doesn't have enough words or the right kind of words to make it plain. It's really too much to get my mind around. But hope for our phoenix day has to be enormous. It must be cosmic in its dimensions. It must be eternal in its time. The source of its energy must be inexhaustible.

It seems that it has always been that way with hope. Look at the seers of other dead ages, who were caught up with phoenix visions for new days. They spoke in figures, in analogies. They wrote in poetry with metaphors and similes. Their words could not contain, or describe, or define the hope they saw and felt; they could only point beyond themselves to the larger reality of the enormity of hope.

Isaiah lived with the suffering of his people. It was not the scene in which hope is usually enacted. But, on the narrow stage, with all its impenetrable limits, hope *was* acted out. It had not come as some force against suffering; it was not a hero sent to rescue, bravely, those who were hurting. Hope came from *suffering.* It was a fantastic, weird idea upon the stage, a prototype theater of the absurd. Hope became a reality through suffering. This was, indeed, the whole meaning of suffering; it was the birth pangs of hope.

> Surely he has borne our griefs
>   and carried our sorrows;
> yet we esteemed him stricken,
>   smitten by God, and afflicted.
> But he was wounded for our transgressions,
>   he was bruised for our iniquities;
> upon him was the chastisement that
>   made us whole,
> and with his stripes we are healed.
>
> —Isaiah 53:4-5

How can you define like that? How can it be put into practical terms? It can't be grasped, understood like a chemical formula, but it was hope for a hurting prophet and his people. Shapeless, formless hope!

Ezekiel knew the fire and ashes of an age dying and dead. His scene of hope has a Halloween feeling to it. There were bones, dried-up bones, everywhere—a valley full of dead men's bones. He saw skulls, ankles, fingers, spines. No serious shrink would have let Ezekiel walk out of his office. He said he saw the bones rattle and clank over themselves. They hooked together—toe to foot to ankle to leg. Whole skeletons stood up, flopping their arms about. Sinew and muscle and skin grew over them. They were ghoulish figures without life. Then the prophet screamed at the wind, and the wind became their breath. Now the "things" turned into people, color in their cheeks, expressions of feelings reflected on their faces. Alive! Glory! Hallelujah!

In such a fashion, Ezekiel brought hope, in his senseless, impractical vision. Hope!

Jeremiah saw the Lord God in a lawyer's office, tearing up the old contract, writing a new one, a contract that would make God much closer to the people, an intimate contract, guaranteeing the Holy Presence with the people—signed, sealed, witnessed, delivered. Hope!

Hope cannot be analyzed in this hazy vision, but we have analyzed other well-defined hopes into oblivion. We have so picked them apart that their parts, like fine flour, have blown away.

Our phoenix day hope needs to be bright in a maze of colors. Fiery reds, exploding in brilliance. Icy cold blues, streaking across black skies. Fantastic yellows that flash in all directions. Greens that live and glow in the dark. Stately purples that pulsate with awe and mystery. Merely black and white hope, described in definite terms, like so many instructions for putting together a tool shed, would be, at the least, inappropriate. Let hope be celebrated with colors, but never strictly defined or limited by them.

The New Testament writers, like their Old Testament mentors, wrote strongly, but fuzzily, of hope. Hope had gripped their lives. They were inspired by it; it motivated them to travel in strange and dangerous places. It gave their lives a sense of anticipation. Hope for the New Testament authors was no idle dream for which they longed in languor, incapacitated by lack of the experience of it. It was, instead, a present reality that had overtaken them and had empowered them.

Yet this hope could not be put into specifics. It was not definable in any way that a compulsive grammar teacher would accept. It existed! It was! That was it! And that was all that could be said of it. Of course, its feelings could be described; its source was evident—a person, Jesus Christ. But those with the best of eyesight could not bring it into focus; it remained indistinct. It was distant, but very present; it was not a possession, but it *was* the possessor; it was unweighable, immeasurable, uncountable, but it pointed to the value by which all values are formed. It was hope.

Hope is seen in the New Testament's apocalypses. These kaleidoscopic descriptions of the end times reveal *(apokalupto)* hope. But to take the figures they use as literal predictions is to miss again the fuzzy nature of their understanding of hope. Probably better than most writers, the apocalyptists create a feeling of hope. They stretch our minds with figures and symbols that are bizarre and fantastic.

Jesus' apocalypse (according to Matthew) deals with calamitous times. False teachers lead people into delusion; the coming of the Son of man is like lightning in a thunderstorm; the sun goes dark and the moon becomes blood; stars tumble out of the sky as if they had been hung like lights in a high ceiling. When all these things have shaken the very foundations of our lives, the Son of man will appear. His sign will be seen in the sky (the cross?). With blazing clouds of brilliance, he will appear. Angels will appear to trumpet together all the chosen from the "four winds" and all across the sky

(Matthew 24:23-31). What is to be made of this? If the symbols become ends in themselves, we have missed the indescribable hope. It becomes revenge time for all those impious persons who have not paid attention to our evangelizing. God will show them! But to read this concern of Jesus in its apocalyptic and symbolic idiom is to sense that in the most horrible of times, when tragedy and uncertainty have done their worst, hope is still a possibility, for the Son of man does, indeed, come into our fallen worlds to redeem and restore "the elect," i.e., those he has chosen. And we are *all* "the chosen."

They are always coming for us, these end times, these apocalyptic days. It is written into the rhythm of our living, just as surely as day and night, the cold winter, the hot summer. It is the systolic and diastolic beating of our society's heart. They are scary times, and calling them a "rhythm" is not to take away the fear and the uncertainty. And it is certainly not to play lightly with our apocalyptic feelings.

But the point of the apocalyptists in the Bible is not to declare that the terrible and terrifying times are about to burst onto the scene. They are already upon us. From Ezekiel's visions, to those of the writer of Revelation, the message is hope. Again, the content of that hope was not clear; it was unfocused; it was ill-defined, and deliberately so. The sense of this hope is seen in one of the servant songs in Isaiah:

> Which of you fears the LORD and obeys his servant's
> commands?
> The man who walks in dark places with no light,
> yet trusts in the name of the LORD and leans on his God.
>
> —Isaiah 50:10 (NEB)

"In dark places with no light. . . ." That is faith. That is hope, hope in the dark, hope unseen.

Why *can't* we see the hope? Why *can't* it be put down in black and white, with fine-pointed pens, with to-the-letter specifications? If hope is real (and not some dream caused by onions and beans eaten at night), then why *can't* it come out into the light and be recognized and examined? Why *must* it always be unweighable, uncountable, unmeasurable?

If we mean, by this hope, the ultimate fulfillment, the purpose behind all God's planning, the last and most magnificent realization of all, it becomes, by definition, undefinable, and moves into that realm in which we are strangers—eternity. How can we ever begin to conceptualize the meaning of meanings, the purpose of purposes, the end of ends, the hope beyond which there can be no more hopelessness? It is quite beyond our minds to concoct an image of the last and ultimate realization.

Is there an ultimate heartbeat, some grand thump that ushers us into the full attainment of the All? If there is, it is very difficult to wrap our minds around it! Sometimes our hearts race with excitement or with exhaustion. They pound away with startling experiences or with anticipation. They beat steadily with the regularity of our routine days. They slow with our sleeping times. Our apocalyptic days are such rhythms. The measure of the grimness of our days is the measure of our need of hope. Some days, finding another shoestring will do it; for other days, it is to scream into the other world and demand, "Hello, is anybody there? Do you care about me?" So—our ultimate hope. Would we dare possess it if we could? Own it in its totality?

It is, perhaps, not that there is such ultimate hope, but rather, that there is always hope, hope of shoestrings and pennies, of passing grades and promotions, of healings and wholeness. That hope is always shapeless; its colors are bright, but changing; its size is both that of an atom and of the universe; its speed exceeds that of light by half again and leaves not even a blur for our eyes. It simply cannot be seen or examined.

> Now hope that is seen is not hope. For who hopes for what he sees? But if we hope for what we do not see, we wait for it with patience (Romans 8:24-25).

If we want any lesser hope, is it hope at all?

We'll Take the Money

The toothy TV emcee was, of course, *en mode,* mod, and all that. He did not have the greasy look, but his personality had a greasy feel; it fairly oozed an oily charm, as phony as the pot of gold set in the background.

The microphone that he kept close to his lips, seemed, somehow, to sustain him, like an intravenous apparatus. Every so often he teased the couple he was interviewing, with a quick pointing of the mike in their faces, only to clutch it back to himself and play on the words they had just spoken into it.

"And now, folks, the big moment is here." (to the couple) "The choice is yours. Do you think you can cool your wowing, zapping nerves enough to choose? Huh? Can you simmer it down, Susie?" (Her name was Susan.)

"Yes, I think so."

"And how about old shiny dome?" (He was bald.) Say, did you ever think of applying for a job as a state capitol?" (guffaws) "Ha, ha." (puts his arm around "Baldy's" shoulder) "You just make the right choice, answer the question, and zappo! No more job applying, anywhere."

"That'd be great."

"Did you hear that? *DID you hear that?* 'It'd be great,' he says." (ripple of laughter as "Baldy" shifts weight to the other foot)

"Okay. Time's running out. Have you chosen? Do you agree?"

Susan looked at "Baldy." They had never met before. Now, it was obvious that if they had agreed, they had not determined who'd do the talking.

"Take one more look at that pot of gold. Around the world! A thirty-five-foot cabin cruiser! And! And! Twenty-five thousand—that's thousands, folks—smackeroos!"

He wheeled around like a retired ballet dancer; then he shoved the microphone under Susan's nose.

"What'll it be, Suzy-Q? Have to hurry; we are running out of tick-tock."

"Uh, well, we, uh, decided to go for the money."

"How about that, Chief Bald Eagle? Do you agree with little brown-eyed Susan?" (Her eyes were blue.)

"Yep, go for the money."

"Okay, here it is—" (He made a gesture with his non-mike arm that was like a windmill.) "Twenty-five big ones!" (He took a card from one of his lackeys, who came and went with a fixed, determined smile.)

"Who was president when the Mississippi, St. Paul, and Oscaloosa Railroad was laid through the mountains of Kansas?"

"Uh, gee, I don' . . ."

"Baldy" grabbed Susan. They went into a huddle with three seconds on the clock, and just as the raspberry buzzer blew its tongue at the nation—

"Martin Van Buren!" It was "Baldy's" desperate voice, choked and squealy.

"Oh, no. I'm soooo sorry!"

The smiley man suddenly became as solicitous as a funeral director, and now it was sympathy, thick as molasses, that oozed from his mask of sorrow. Then, suddenly, he wheeled, and as he shot his finger at the TV audience, he shouted: "A word from our sponsor!"

"Our Sponsor" was a *femme fatale.* "I know what you want—a lively, thrilling sex life, right?" Then followed an announcement about a miracle toothpaste that outdoes all that the potions of ancient India had promised.

Off camera, "Baldy" and Susan went to separate seats with a year's supply of the sexy toothpaste. If anyone had wanted to know the answer to that tidbit of history, they went to bed with a hungry curiosity.

6 We'll Take the Money

It seems stupid in our society to ask: What do you want? It's so obvious. Coal miners, schoolteachers, and airline pilots have been on strike. Why? Mostly for the money. E. F. Hutton speaks; the world stops in its tracks, as if it were some stop-action scene, in order to learn the secret. What secret? How to make money. I take a young, wounded softball warrior to the emergency room, where he's checked, pronounced okay, and sent home. The bill? It was $76, which had to be paid before we left.

It would seem that the one thing that we are living for, planning for, working for, is money. It is as if our society had become hooked on a drug, and the habit is insatiable. It has become our *sine qua non.* It is our *raison d'être.* It is (to borrow Tillich's phrase) our "ultimate concern." More than a medium of exchange, it has become our god.

Most choices are fuzzy, not very clear-cut, a lot of gray—now whitish, now blackish. But one option is clearly yes or no, right or wrong, black or white. Jesus pointed it out. There is the Lord God, and there is money (mammon). Both are masters, but no one can be servant of both. Which shall it be: God or money?

Thank you, we have made our choice. It seems an odd quirk that on all our currency we have stamped or imprinted: "In God We Trust." Our motto may indicate our ambivalence, but our choice seems obvious—we'll take the money!

What is money that it has become the object of this voracious hunger of ours? It is a mysterious, hidden, transcendent quality that makes it even more godlike. We rarely see it. We hold some paper from time to time, but we are warned that carrying too much of the greenback stuff is not smart. My bank sends me a statement each month, advising me (if I'm lucky) that there is a balance on hand. Perhaps, but I've never seen it. Where is this balance? And the green paper is not really money; it represents money, a sort of generally accepted symbol of wealth. It's not necessarily swappable for a silver buck, "on demand of bearer," and the silver dollar is no longer silver, anyway. I am paid by a check; I pay my bills by check. Neither I nor my creditors ever see *money.* Our unseen, all-powerful, little god. As the hymn writer put it:

> Immortal, invisible, God only wise,
> In light inaccessible hid from our eyes. . . .
> —Walter Chalmers Smith, "Immortal, Invisible, God Only Wise"

At the risk of sacrilege and irreverence for the divine dollar, I want to ask what it is, that we should have it our end-all? It is, of course, not a god. Of itself, it is nothing. Cash in all your bonds; draw all the money out of your bank account; sell your house for the real money (whatever that may be); pile it up and look at it. It can, by itself, do nothing for you, except put your life in jeopardy. But that's the way it is when you fool around in the presence of phony divinity. If all that loot is to mean anything to you, you have to dangle it out in front of someone and get him or her to dance to your tune. People will take it in order to beat out the rhythm for someone else. The money, completely passive, simply gets passed on and on and on. By itself, it does absolutely nothing. So what is this nothing for which we sweat, hurt, push, shove, lie, scheme, kill?

For one thing, money is a meter by which we measure how much we want something.

Before I had gotten around to the price tag, I had decided I wanted the tie. The plaid was the official tartan for my Scottish ancestors' clan. It was bright, and I sort of fancied walking about with this ancient symbol flapping in front of me. An emblem. A flag. An identity. Then I found it, hidden behind the folds in the back—the price! Twelve bucks! (That was back in 1976.) I wouldn't be much of a Scotsman to spend that much on a tie. Money (again the mysterious, unseen, inaccessible) determined how much I wanted the tie.

Some sort of internal calculator measures the wanting against the price, and we find out just how much we want the whatever. Of course, merchants know the tricks of "the sale." It was a twelve-dollar tie. No doubt about that, I saw the price. The worth equalled all those things twelve dollars would have bought—a steak dinner for two in a not-too-fancy restaurant, a tank of gas(!), a couple of packs of film. Now, with the twelve-dollar tag stuck in my mind, more tightly than on the tie, when I came back after Christmas and saw, "Reduced for clearance—$7.95," wow, what a bargain! For seven-ninety-five, the tie was in proportion to the gas, steak, film, and I was inclined to buy it. "It was a steal," I exclaimed apologetically to my wife. "This is a twelve-dollar tie!" I wanted the tie when I measured it beside all the seven-ninety-five buys, but not when I measured it with twelve-dollar items.

Such a measuring rod should be *God* for me?

It is a way of measuring, determining worth (metric, at that), but it is also power. (OK, now you are beginning to sound like you are talking of God, almighty, powerful, omnipotent.)

Money is the out-held carrot that all asses seek. Dangle enough in front of them, and they will pull almost any load. It is the instrument of manipulation and control. It brings loyalty and devotion to the priest who parcels out this sacrament. The boss, the company, the contract—all come before family, friends, and the fatherland. Long hours. Double-time, overtime. Days in lonely motels. Tension. Ulcers. Hypertension. Modern priests with the holy sacrament in their possession can, and often do, demand such sacrifices of their devotees. Money empowers a pagan priesthood of people manipulators.

Part of its power is that of enabling. It helps good things happen. It sends a child off to college and returns (maybe) an adult with skills and data that offer possibilities for fulfillment.

It broadens our acquaintance with the world, a palliative for the itchy-foot syndrome. Romantic Italy! Charming France! Historic Britain! Mysterious India! You can come home and do the slide-show circuit for six months.

It offers the promise of health: spas and athletic clubs, special diets and organic foods, vitamins and slimming potions. If you are at the coping level of health, downers and uppers can be had for a price, or counselors and psychiatrists. And, of course, "a trip to Florida, for my health, you know." If you are at the hurting level—doctors and specialists, tests and X rays, hospitals and operations.

Some guest on a talk show, whom I have long since forgotten, said of money, "It is a good lubricant for the machinery of life." To wit, it enables some things to happen.

Money is security. It is characteristic of the gods that if they are pleased with us, they will protect us. For some (not all), a little money in the rainy-day account makes life feel better. "Just in case, you know."

Beyond the rainy-day money, we buy what-if protection, because we can dream up all sorts of disasters that might find us without protection. What if we get sick? What if my house burns up? What if I die with a family to support? Some call it insurance. It calms our what-if fears with an officially decorated document written in some other language. For money we are given protection from the "acts of God," i.e., that other God with the big "G."

A farmer friend in Iowa has no insurance. If the crops are crushed by hail, so be it. If his house burns to ashes, that's it. If his health breaks and his hospital expenses are too great, well that's tough. He told me that you either trust insurance for security, or God. It was a mammon—God choice for him. He knows we don't see eye to eye on insurance, but he is right: life has to be more than some compulsive concern for security. I can't buy his reasoning, but I admire his guts.

Money is identity, too. It says something about who one is. And the more one has, the louder it is said.

"Is he anybody?"

"Is he anybody! Don't you know who he is? That's Fletcher T. Biltmore. He has millions!"

To have it, millions or less, is to be recognized as successful. Within that identity there are all kinds of sought-after qualities: ambitious, assertive, skilled, knowledgeable, intelligent, capable, powerful, strong. The successful man is the man with *macho.* The woman who makes it is liberated. Who am I? Ask my automobiles, my houses, my clothes, my securities. Money is identity.

My money can also identify me as good. Harvey Katz points out in his book *Give! Who Gets Your Charity Dollar?* that we Americans give away more than $55 million a day. He further notes that this figure does not include the thousands upon thousands of hours of volunteer work done for these institutions to which we contribute so generously.[1] We are generous and, therefore, good. But, we expect goodness of our religion, don't we? An ancient and honorable tradition is that religion offers ways to deal with our guilt. Even for us who trust in God and lean on mammon, there is the possibility of goodness.

Churches and charities who have made the impossible peace between God and mammon make implicit promises of goodness for contributions (with tax deductions, of course). I recently received one of those "Dear Alumnus/a" letters. It asked for information for an "alumni/ae" directory. There was a deluxe edition to be had for $25; the also-ran edition was $17.50. However, if I contributed $50, I would not only receive the deluxe edition, but also my name would be listed in the directory with the special contributors. The gimmick has many variations. "Loyal alumni/ae"—$25 and above, up to $100. Then, "Extra-Effort alumni/ae"—up to $500. "In-depth supporters"—up to $1,000. Finally, "The President's Club"—above $1,000. (I picture a walnut-paneled room with chandeliers and waiters serving Scotch.)

Goodness is etched into art in churches. "To the glory of God and in memory of J. Bilton Bonk III." Stained glass, chancel furniture, organs, it's all there—a little purchased goodness.

Where would our institutions be without it, all this "goodness" money? Lost, naturally. Does it do any good, that is, besides making someone good? Obviously, it does. Hospitals are built and equipped. Colleges and universities expand and faculties are paid (however poorly). Food, medical help, and housing for victims of disaster save lives in such crises. Money does a lot of good, and part of the good it does is to bestow some goodness on the one who had it to give in the first place.

Money at the rock-bottom line is exchange, or to be more precise and economically correct—it is a medium of exchange. It is value for value, this for that, dollars for eggs. Most of us give time (life), skills (personal know-how), effort (our own energies) in exchange for this stuff we, in turn, exchange for meat and potatoes, housing and utilities, clothes and cars, and whatever, if there is any left over.

All of which is to say that if money is our god, then it doesn't "Emmanuel" (God-with-us) with us very long. This god is always leaving us or it is not doing the job for us. It is only power for us when we let it go; it only performs its enabling act as we give it up. If we hold on to this mammon, we could starve, freeze, go naked, not go at all. Give it up, or it is nothing; when we do give it up, we have nothing, except, of course, that for which we gave it up. But the power and possibility of the cash is gone with the giving up.

If what concerns us ultimately is our god, and if money is our ultimate concern, it is some strange god we have—it is powerful only as we exchange it. Is it this money that we really want more than anything else? Yet what enormous sacrifices we lay down for it!

Obviously, money is not what ultimately concerns us; it is what money in our possession can do. It can enable us to own cars, take trips, obtain tutoring (whether or not we get an education in the process does not depend on the money), buy land and houses—all that. Money, in fact, enables us to be morally sound in a society based on a consuming ethic. All religions pretty much have their set of commands, ethics, moral dos and don'ts. If money is our ultimate concern, our want of wants, our god, then its demands of us are gathered from the new Sinai, Wall Street, and have to do with consuming.

Consumerism is not only a way of expressing our devotion, but also it is a way of spreading the faith, to wit—witnessing. If I keep buying cars (American or foreign), a vacant spot happens on the dealer's lot. He orders a new car. People keep working on the assembly line. Delivery is made. The spot is filled. All along the line money has been kept in circulation, and I have fulfilled my duty, blessing the dealer, the manufacturer, the transporters, the workers involved, the government people, the salesperson, whose pious, seductive ability to conclude the sale started the whole process off in the first place. The blessings do not end here. What can be said for all the suppliers of paint, steel, plastic, fabric, batteries, tires, electrical doodads, etc.? And, once again, the blessings fan out to the transporters, the government people, and a host of lesser and unknown fellow worshipers of our common ultimate concern.

The wise hierarchy of our faith has seen that the process does not crack down in any serious way and has, by its divine wisdom, built obsolescence into all this stuff. Vance Packard made us all aware of this renewing blessing back in the 1960s.[2] Apparently, since then, we have opted to increase our devotion to this expression of our ultimate concern.

The evil to be avoided is that old ethic (often called Protestant) that respected and applauded saving. We have succeeded not only in making saving something less ethical than consuming, but also we have made it stupid. The going rate for "saving" is always just below the going rate for inflation, so that we are faced with the paradox (and what religion worth its salt would be without paradoxes?): Saving will cost you money!

In this new faith there is a sort of eschatology called credit; that is, it has to do with the future and fulfillment. But in the faith of monetary Ultimate Concern, the new eschatology has them reversed: fulfillment and future. Or the more familiar, "Fly now, pay later" verse. The event of fulfillment is not 'way off there in the never-never land of last things. It is now. Buy now. Have now. Possess now. There is still one point in which the old and new eschatologies have a minor agreement; the judgment *is* in the future. Debts, like deeds, do have a way of coming due for judgment (payment).

In the old faith Paul talked about an *arrabon,* an earnest, a promise, a down payment. He thought of it as that which the Lord God gave us, a sort of taste of what the full banquet would be like. In the new ultimate concern the *arrabon* is that which the consumer offers the credit divinity. This does not obligate the god to him or her (as in Paul's old-fashioned idea); it, rather, obligates the devotee to the god. In fact, credit is a way of laying claim to our lives. We buy on "time payments." Time is the stuff our lives are made of; we are, then, paying for our stuff with hunks of our lives, our time.

The question is: Is this what we want, the way we want to live? Is consumerism the real reflection of our value system? Is this merry-go-round as merry as we can know? Is working-buying-having-working-buying *(ad infinitum)* our Ultimate Concern? If it is, congratulations! We have arrived (or are in the process of arriving). Let's keep up the good work-buy-have-work-buy cycle. Most of our society will offer us extraordinary support. There is credit, and if we get in over our heads, the heavenly parent will assist us through the courts of bankruptcy. Our neighbors will understand (perhaps not love) us, and we can have the assurance that our life-style is a perfectly acceptable one, threatening no one, affirming many. We will be looked upon as solid citizens, especially if we "buy American." When the holy oracle from Wall Street has had a bullish day, we will know that in some small way, we have made a positive contribution. We can celebrate the old, but rebaptized holy days, and feel the same old glow we knew at Christmas time in the old faith, which faded because it kept giving confusing signals about sacrifice, that weird idea.

If work-buy-have-etc. is "where it's at" for you, don't read any further. What follows may seem sinister and subversive, and it is probably (in terms of the new faith) x-ratedly obscene.

Remember *Games People Play?* It was another hot item in the book department in the sixties. The author, Eric Berne, was high on honesty, being straightforward, and open. Games were a way of being evasive, of living with ulterior motives. They were also ways of pleasing others, of avoiding the honest and hard struggle of genuine relationships. Games were responses of one who had some idea of what others wanted. So one played out these games. All the gamey stuff actually avoids what one wants more than anything else—avoids it because these concerns are risky, demand some assertiveness, and, above all, honesty. None of these commodities, that Berne recognized as deep inner longings, can be had for money—not at any price. They can be had for a different exchange which is not passed on and lost, as money is. The price: courage, openness, and assuming responsibility for one's self. The commodities are awareness, spontaneity, and intimacy.[3]

What do we want? What is our Ultimate Concern? Something more than money. Dollars are not enough. Perhaps it is something very like Berne's awareness: learning, growing, having one's consciousness raised. All of this could spread out in different directions: awareness of one's self, of one's environment, of one's "beyond." What is more than money? "What is more" could very well be spontaneity: joy, openness, expressing one's honest feelings, responding out of one's self, instead of what everybody else expects. It could be something to be had, something that dollars can't buy; it could be intimacy, the genuine article, not just the body-rubbing sort, but the soul-rubbing variety, really making it with someone who mattered and who cared, experiencing closeness as a way of living, instead of an overnight stand.

Neither Berne nor Freud, neither Moses nor Elijah, neither Carter nor Breshnev can finally express the bottom line for any of us. That decision is ours alone, each of us. I'm betting my Adam's apple that for all of us it is more than money, this Ultimate Concern of ours; and what's more (what a gambler!), my bet is that it is more than the stuff money can buy.

If I'm right, then we are really in a bind, all of us. I want to be warm (cool in the summer) and have lights in my house. Oh, yes, my house, I want one of those, too. It will need painting this year, and I need to replace the shrubs in front. I'm not too fond of hunger; I mean, if I starve, that's no great help to the starving, is it? Modesty and low temperatures combine to make nude living an embarrassing and cold experience, for which I am not ready. I am gaining some of Berne's "awareness"; I need money!

We began with a clear-cut decision—mammon or God, money or the Lord. Are we now winding up with some irresolvable conflict? Mammon as god or the Lord as God. The decision is easy; living it out is the bind.

Some have opted out of it all. Go to the islands and live off the land. (Of course, it took some sort of cash to get there.) Ride the rails and become a part of America's heroic hoboes. Drop out of responsibility and let the responsible ones take care of you. Get into a commune—all for one, one for all, all that sort of thing. Become a monk and live in contemplation in a monastery (try Our Lady of Gethsemane in Kentucky—it's beautiful). These are ways to beat the bind of dealing with money needs and deeper wants, and some of the above may be just the thing.

Probably most of us are in the "none of the above" category; but possibly we are not in the money-as-Ultimate-Concern class either.

All of which lands us back in old and familiar territory—*what do we want?* It has the feeling of Berne's "awareness." If it is not money and the stuff that it buys, then what?

It is an act of faith to move from that territory. There are old and familiar scenes there; there are also old and familiar ruts that go round and round the same scenery. It feels comfortable, secure here, boring, but secure. Leaving what feels like protection (plodding along from day to day without ever having to know what one wants) is risky business. One has to be convinced that staying *here* is to miss something *there.* So "what do you want?" can be a scary question. It's beginning to have the feel of an Abram, walking along the wall of Ur, wondering what's out there.

The act of faith becomes indeed an act when there is something inside that trusts that finding a more-than-money purpose is possible, that it really exists out there, somewhere beyond the walls. One becomes convinced, slowly or suddenly. New directions happen—not toward the islands, the freight trains, The Confrere Commune, or even Our Lady of Gethsemane. The real beginning and the real leaving are not geographical. It is to believe that I belong to Someone other than the greed stuff. It is to begin to explore what that means with the faith that its meaning has to do with reality—with one's inner reality and with one's environmental reality. It means accepting a life-style that is simple and making simplicity the unmoving hub, instead of the beginning from which one must move, in order to possess stuff.

It means hearing with a new and personal intensity Jesus' parable:

> And he told them a parable, saying, "The land of a rich man brought forth plentifully; and he thought to himself 'What shall I do, for I have nowhere to store my crops?' And he said, 'I will do this; I will pull down my barns, and build larger ones; and there I will store all my grain and my goods. And I will say to my soul, Soul, you have ample goods laid up for many years; take your ease, eat, drink, be merry.' But God said to him, 'Fool! This night your soul is required of you; and the things you have prepared, whose will they be?' So is he who lays up treasures for himself, and is not rich toward God" (Luke 12:16-21).

It's Hell to Want

"Your wants will consume you alive.

"They will gnaw at your entrails like a greedy cancer.

"They will finally leave you emaciated, weak, begging for death to strike you."

The preacher's head was beaded with droplets of perspiration. The naked light bulb just over his head created a glowing halo which seemed to pulsate with the heat. The whole church was hot, and I had the fantasy that from the outside it glowed in the night, like a red-hot coal. God's judgment was on fire, and the heat of it was touching us all, on that humid Mississippi July night.

"Them lusts that burn in the loins—you know what I mean—are the will of the Devil come alive in your very body!

"They are the dry rot of hell that will eat out your soul.

"And you will only be a body of uncontrollable wants that will lead you around like you had a ring in your nose.

"You'll be dead, but your body will be alive, filled with a hunger and a thirst that you can't satisfy.

"It is all because of your sinful and evil wants.

"They all have to be pulled out and replaced by God's holy will!"

It felt like a call to become eunuchs, and some strange hookup in my mind brought back horrible memories of childhood fears.

"You, you lustful-eyed husband—

"HEAR ME—

"You let your sinful eyeballs wander away from that dear bride.

"You swore to be faithful and loyal.

"Now, she's old, and you're tired of her.

"DO YOU HEAR ME?

"I know what you want, and your wants are dragging your soul straight to Hell.

"You, you young, filthy filly, with your short dresses and tight sweaters—

"LISTEN TO ME!

"You, that God made in the crystal image of the lily-white purity of the Virgin Mary herself.

"You can never get that back—NO, NEVER—YOU HEAR ME?

"I know what you want, and your wants will drive you into a devil's arms, and you'll get passed on from devil to devil,

"Until you wind up in Satan's arms and spend eternity in the rot and stench of Hell.

"You, you mean, bloodshot-eyed booze guzzler—

"DON'T YOU TURN YOUR HEAD AWAY—

"I know what you want.

"You *know* I know what you want.

"All that slop is beginning to wiggle and move in your head.

"It's turning to worms, and it's eating out your brains.

"You think you've felt its fire in your belly.

"Oh, brother, you ain't felt no burning yet!

"When the fires of Hell take over your innards, all the Alka-Seltzer in the world won't put out that never-ending flame.

"NOW, YOU GET THIS IN YOUR HEAD—EVERY ONE OF YOU:

"It's *your* wishes, it's *your* desires, it's *your* wants; and they're sending you to Hell on Special Delivery.

"Your wants will damn your soul to the hottest Hell of all.

"Your wants will burst into flame, and you'll scream in pain for all eternity."

At the point of climax, the preacher, still snorting out the dangers of wanting, came down out of the pulpit. He motioned to the choir to sing, and as they began a slow, quiet hymn, he told us to come forward and lay all our wants on the altar and be healed of their terrifying consequences.

"THE LORD IS YOUR SHEPHERD. YOU MUST NOT WANT!"

7 Rotten at the Core

There's a ghost out of my past that comes to haunt me at this point. This specter would not agree with the thesis of this book and is not happy about what has been said to this point. His censoring voice comes off an old tape that is spinning in my head, right now. He may be your ghost, too. Anyway, I want to deal with him—gently, if possible (I *am* a peaceable sort), but honestly, realistically, straight on.

This ghost got programmed into my growing-up process, but he began for our clan in a hundred different places, but probably in much the same circumstances. He was resurrected by ancestors for whom life had become too much. Changes had come too thick and fast to be understood, measured, or dealt with. Certainties about life and death, on the other hand, became fewer and dearer. Then, the ancestors, like their children, became haunted with the idea that they were, themselves, essentially evil. Strip off all the outer niceties, all the politeness, the simple kindnesses, right down to the core of it all, and one would find an undiluted cesspool of evil, corruption, and wickedness. The theologians had diagnosed them as "totally depraved." Obviously depraved people with no virtue, no real intelligence, no important strengths could not be expected to cope with life. They gave up in the face of their overwhelming depravity.

Of course, the situation was not without hope (or so it seemed). There were various theological obstacle courses that offered some unclear promises of escape from one's wicked inner core. But the theologians, competing for prominence, had different maps for the way through the course, and individuals were left to be influenced by one or the other. Some, feeling that their salvation depended on loyalty to their mentor, defended that mentor to the death (sometimes, quite literally). But of one certainty, as real as the foundations of the church house, one could be sure—rotten at the core!

Well, I must admit, I have caricatured "total depravity." And, what is probably worse, I have exaggerated the persons who had to do with it. It's difficult to be all that objective about a tenet I cannot accept. I want to call on someone else who is more kindly disposed to this belief, to explain it. But first, what does depravity have to do with *Wanting, Becoming, Believing?*

I have assumed that to know our wants at their deepest level is to know ourselves at the core. Wants come bubbling up from the depths of us, not altogether consciously and often disguised (viz., the sex urge is not simply an appetite for orgasm; it is a desire for a relationship of the most intimate and enduring sort).

If the core of us, the beginning place of our wants, is rotten, evil, thoroughly wicked, then obviously our wants can hardly be heaven-sent wishes for goodness. If the birthing place for our wants is a womb of such unspeakable filth and evil, our wants are obviously part of that depravity, and the end result of our taking them seriously is the most horrible destruction that can be conjured out of our corrupted imaginations. Such wanting could not possibly be an act of faith; it would be, instead, an act of evil, of disbelief, of despair, and of horror. Wanting would then be the source of all that could bring disgrace, terror, shame, or condemnation to the one who mistakenly allowed himself or herself to be guided by what is wanted. Wants would be the very lures by which one is seduced into all those despicable acts that destroy decency, love, lovers, and one's self.

From the core of us, nothing good could arise, nothing that would heal, that would care, that would redeem, that would reconcile. The thoroughly depraved *esse* of us all would be that dreadful human burden we are all called on to tote about, like some grotesque growth on the souls of us whose malignancy will yet consume our lives.

All of which is to say, that there is an either-or fork in this road; at least, that appears to be the case. At any rate, let's deal with this ancient ghost.

My prejudices are out in the open. I simply don't buy total depravity at all. I don't think it is biblical. I believe it is destructive. I am convinced that it is a fear of life that denies us life. It would probably be expecting too much to suppose that there will be a lot of objectivity in my dealing with this doctrine, but I'll try. And I'll begin by looking to some others who see truth in this view of persons as essentially evil.

Augustine seems a likely theologian of substance with whom to begin. The famous fourth-century bishop of Hippo, in North Africa, was not always a pure and pious person. In his youth, Augustine was quite a high flyer. In his late teens he had his own concubine, one of those perquisites for people of means. When Augustine first began to be attracted toward Christianity, realizing that such a commitment meant giving up his indulgent life-style, he prayed, rather half-heartedly, for divine control for his desires: "Lord, make me continent, but not yet." When Augustine made his decision for Christ, however, he did give up his womanizing life-style.

He had heard the great Chrysostom preach, and perhaps he was influenced by the famous preacher's ideas about sinfulness in people. Chrysostom saw Adam's fall as opening a pathway to all who followed him, but because of freedom, people could choose either path. Augustine went further.

In fact, he went further than all his mentors. All the church fathers were aware of human sinfulness and of the unlimited variations on that theme. They did not, however, believe humankind to be essentially and thoroughly evil. It was just as obvious that humans had the capability of turning from evil to the good. The choice was one's own. Salvation dealt with the effects of the sins already committed and with the propensity to repeat them.

Augustine was restless with this either-or, sin-or-goodness choice. For him, it was not a question of choice; it was a matter of the nature of humanity. And he saw that nature as essentially evil. For him, there were no inherent capabilities for good in humankind. Only Adam was created with the will to choose good or evil. When he elected to choose the wrong, he polluted himself, became mortal, and passed his sinful nature on to all generations who followed. It is far more than coincidence (my own biased opinion) that this man, who had become obsessed over his sexual life-style, should believe that this total depravity is passed on from one generation to the other in the sex act. Fisher wrote about Augustine's view of sexuality: "This [sexual] appetite is itself the fruit of the first sin, as well as the means whereby the sinful nature is communicated from father to son."[1]

Augustine's "depravity" did not go unchallenged. Pelagius, a church father of lesser note, created a stir of controversy with the great bishop of Hippo. Pelagius felt that humankind was mortal, simply because it was created that way. It was not Adam's sin, he believed, that caused humankind, for all time, to be less than immortal. If humans are sinners, they are sinners by their own choices, as was Adam. Pelagius felt that humans are thoroughly capable of good and evil acts. At birth, people are only what God has made them, and the assumption that evil is the core reality within the newborn is monstrous. Persons are what they determine to be, and each bears the consequences of his or her choices.

I'm for Pelagius, but it was Augustine who won the day.

Over a millennium later, Augustine's view was fertile ground for Luther and Calvin to plant seeds of total depravity and declare that all that was human was evil.

The Westminster Confession reflected Calvin's influence:

> Our first parents . . . so became dead in sin and wholly defiled in all faculties and parts of soul and body. They being the root of all mankind, the guilt of this sin was imputed, and the same death in sin and corrupted nature conveyed, to all their posterity . . . whereby we are utterly indisposed, disabled, and made opposite to all good, and wholly inclined to all evil. . . .[2]

And, further in the same confession,

> "Man by his fall into a state of sin, hath wholly lost all ability of will to any spiritual good accompanying salvation; so as a natural man, being altogether averse from that good, and dead in sin, is not able, by his own strength, to convert himself, or to prepare himself there unto."[3]

These puritans left no loopholes!

A twentieth-century reflection of Augustine's and Calvin's doctrines comes from John Murray's article in the *Twentieth Century Encyclopedia of Religious Knowledge.* "Depravity" is alive and well for this modern writer.

Murray's rationale is biblical. He has us turn to Genesis 6:5, the prelude to the great deluge: ". . . the wickedness of man was great in the earth, and . . . every imagination of the thoughts of his heart was only evil continually." There are many other biblical citations. From these references, Murray concludes, "The implications respecting the *intensity, inwardness, inclusiveness, exclusiveness,* and *continuousness* of the evil are to be distinctly noted." (Emphasis mine.) And Murray spells out just what these implications are:

1. Humans have nothing of themselves with which to please God.
2. They are, in fact, God's enemy.
3. Such is not the condition of the "few," but the "all."
4. The condition, like the effects of our parents' genes, is inherited.
5. While depravity is total for all, some show it off more than others.
6. The only way out is to be "born again," regenerated.

Murray's grim conclusion is: "To try to evade the conclusion that depravity is total would be futile. Man as depraved is destitute of all that is well-pleasing to God. . . ."[4]

Augustine would be proud. Calvin would applaud.

John M. Krumm's refreshing book, *The Art of Being a Sinner,* puts it in a better perspective:

> We must not exaggerate . . . what the Christian tradition means when it talks about sin as our natural condition. It cannot mean that there is nothing good about us at all. If one means by "total depravity" that there is not a scrap of goodness in man at all, then it is a logical contradiction. If men were totally depraved, they would be so bad they would not even be aware they were bad.[5]

Murray is certainly aware that humankind is bad, but, then, Krumm would say such awareness isn't all bad, because it would tell us that we aren't all good, either. "And that ain't bad!"

Paul Ricoeur asks a more disturbing question. If the Bible really sees us as totally defiled, then why the rituals for cleansing? These washings are surely symbolic; so it must follow that whatever they wash out is symbolic, as well. So perhaps depravity is a symbol. It says that we need to take seriously our capacity for evil. It does not say we are totally depraved.[6]

So where are we? The bottom line is: Can we trust our wants? Or are they seductive whispers, from our essential depravity, luring us to a lurid destruction?

If we are not totally depraved (and here's my vote that we're not!), surely no one would seriously make a case for our being totally "praved" (or whatever the opposite side of the coin may be). The long, sorry history of human inhumanity—the capacity for atrocity, for avarice, for unbridled hatred—makes an airtight case against original goodness and light for all humankind. If not Augustine, Calvin, Murray, et al., then at least some of the Greek fathers and

Pelagius may make sense; humans can obviously do wrong, have done wrong, and in all probability will choose to do it again and again. And they will do it because they will it, choose it, to wit, want to do the wrong.

Now, if the thesis of this book is to float (i.e., that wants are not the undoing of us, but the making of us), then we'd better find some firm footing, some sound ground that will support the claim that paying attention to our wants, understanding them, taking responsibility for them is, in fact, an act of faith, a good, commendable, constructive response to the Lord God.

My first witness is Ezekiel. In the long chain of events encompassed by the stories of Genesis to the exile of Ezekiel and his compatriots, something has been growing, evolving in the human creatures. Men and women are becoming individuals, finding their existence apart from the tribe, the clan, even the family. Ezekiel's keen observation of what is happening, his acute awareness, comes like an oracle from the Lord God:

> The word of the LORD came to me again: "What do you mean by repeating this proverb concerning the land of Israel, 'The fathers have eaten sour grapes, and the children's teeth are set on edge'? As I live, says the Lord GOD, this proverb shall no more be used by you in Israel" (Ezekiel 18:1-3).

Then further: "The soul that sins shall die. The son shall not suffer for the iniquity of the father . . ." (Ezekiel 18:20).

A lot of stuff gets passed along from parent to child. The syndrome of the battered child is a case in point. A boy gets beaten up as he grows up. This behavior gets programmed into his thinking: this is the way you deal with kids—if they don't do your thing, whack 'em. And so on to the next generation. Is this sin evidence of total depravity passed on from generation to generation? Not if we take Ezekiel seriously.

"I can't help it; it was the way I was raised." Ezekiel doesn't buy that kind of "don't blame me" philosophy. We are, all of us, responsible for our choices—for good or bad. If your teeth are set on edge, it was your choice to eat the sour grapes, and you have the consequences you ordered. The choice to live as one is raised, is obviously, an option, but it is a choice one has made. However, it is possible to choose to live differently from the way one was raised.

Ezekiel is beginning to deal with the kind of maturity that enables one to claim one's own life, make choices, and accept the consequences of the decisions. This prophet did not see humankind cursed with a total depravity that would deny persons the freedom and responsibility of their own lives. Whatever the differences of their circumstances might have been, the Old Testament prophets were agreed that people had choices; that is, they could choose to do the right thing. If people were so horribly tainted with original sin, what possible good would be done by preaching at them what God wanted them to do?

In the New Testament, there is little to support the rotten-at-the-core image of humanity.

In the Sermon on the Mount, Jesus obviously has hope that people will excel the righteousness of the scribes and the Pharisees. These folk about whom he had hope were not a select few who had undergone rigorous training in soul and mind, that would make them exceptions to the run-of-the-mill. They were all next-door types, basic, everyday human types.

More than in his sermonizing, Jesus believed in people. Healing is solid evidence that he must have seen something good inside. Why heal a thoroughly rotten person? Healing people who are basically wicked would seem to be defeating the whole purpose of establishing a kingdom for the Lord God. Strong bodies and suppurating souls would make strange citizens for the realm. And if it be argued that Jesus also worked some spiritual cleansing upon those healed, it is strange that most of them were unaware of such changes in themselves. For instance, consider the man who was born blind. (John's story [chapter 9] is instructive in several ways. When asked about the cause of the man's blindness—"Did this man sin, or his parents, that he was born blind?"—Jesus denied that his or his parents' sinfulness had anything to do with his condition.)

The blind man had no comprehension of what had happened to him. The religious authorities had some discussion about the sinfulness of Jesus. The formerly blind man replied that he had no idea whether or not Jesus was a sinner. All he did know was that he was blind, but now he could see! What a marvelous opening it might have been: "I don't know whether or not Jesus is a sinner. I know *I* was, and he cleansed the horrid sinfulness out of my soul." Instead, "I used to be blind, but no more! That's all I know!"

Again, it is John who gives us God's purpose in Jesus' life: "For God so loved the world that he gave his only Son, that whoever believes in him should not perish, but have eternal life"(John 3:16).

If God loved the world to such a degree, and if we worldly creatures are so totally depraved, what does that say about a God to whom such totally perverted people are appealing, desirable? Anyone who is drawn to the rotten-to-the-core kind of people either sees something lovable, something decent, something hopeful, something redeemable, *or* that person has an awfully weird sort of love.

Paul brings the whole human picture into focus in his own struggle. He shared it honestly, openly, with the Roman Christians:

> I do not understand my own actions. For I do not do what I want, but I do the very thing I hate. Now if I do what I do not want, I agree that the law is good. So then it is no longer I that do it, but sin which dwells within me. For I know that nothing good dwells within me, that is, in my flesh. I can will what is right, but I cannot do it (Romans 7:15-18).

First, note that Paul assumes responsibility for the struggle. He had not run away from the inner conflict. It might have been easy to assume that this depraved nature of his is really to blame. Yet he holds himself responsible for what happens (or what does not happen).

Paul would deny that his wishes and will were not good; it was the one good he knew about himself. "I can will what is right. . . ." The good begins in Paul's wanting. He honestly confesses that he cannot bring it about in his own ability alone. Paul's hyperbole is echoed in the Book of Common Prayer's general confession: "There is no health in us." (No wholeness, no completeness.) It is a different cry from no goodness, total depravity. Both the prayer of confession and Paul's statement are prayers for help. But how shall thoroughly wicked people ever come to know that they may pray for divine help, for God's forgiveness?

I want to go back to the Old Testament, to Psalm 8. Its high humanism is hardly that of Augustine, Calvin, or Murray.

> What is man that thou art mindful of him,
> and the son of man that thou dost care for him?
> Yet thou hast made him little less than God,
> and dost crown him with glory and honor.
> —Psalm 8:4-5

These are not words to describe the wretched creature who is totally evil and who is only one of a long descent of those who have received and passed on this depraved nature throughout all the generations of history.

Let's wind up this haunting tale of depravity with a fresh look at Revelation. It comes from David Spangler. He deals with the four horsemen, and our concern will be the first, the white horse, whom Spangler names "Illusion."

To understand Spangler's point, we need to have some understanding of "thought forms." Thought forms which we create are like robots, programmed to do certain things, and to do them continually, until they are out of energy, reprogrammed, or destroyed. Sometimes our emotional deficiencies project thought forms; they create a reality, not as it is, but as we may need it to be in order to deal with it in terms of our emotional inadequacies.

Spangler says that these thought forms create "an excess of baggage which has no relevancy whatsoever to anything that [man] is doing or thinking or attempting to do."

He continues:

> It is purely the product of the past, yet it is highly active and continues to condition man in various ways. This plane, until such time as the human race itself finally meets the test of it and dispels it, will remain as one of the great testers of humanity. It provides the test of discrimination, the test between emotion and intuition.[7]

This thought form, with its excess baggage, Spangler identifies as coming out of the past, a racial memory—original sin. It is this racial memory, he contends, that is the source of imposed suffering. "If I can only suffer enough, I will, in some way, purge this shadow from the land." The suffering complex brings us back to the white horseman, the conquering horseman. He seeks, by suffering and calamity, to purge the world of its original sin, one that can be purged only by destruction of the most massive kind.

To interpret Spangler on a more personal level, I take it that this thought form, original sin/guilt, is self-denial. This is not a self-denial that has to do with discipline and thus rising to a more self-fulfilled life. It is the self-denial that has to do with the shadow side of us, with the genuinely demonic. It is self-punishment for one's original sin/guilt. It becomes some foul-tasting purgative of the spirit that is supposed to clean out the soul of all its filth, but the physic becomes habitual and the cleansing is then less important than the taking of it.

Total depravity declares that we deserve only trouble and distress. We are at home with feelings such as: "This always happens to me," "I might have expected this," "It's never going to get any better," "What's the use!" "Illusion" has us in its clutches. We are rotten at the core; so, naturally, rotten things happen to us. Al Capp helped us look at this ridiculous image with his characteristic humor. Joe Bftsplk, of the Lil' Abner series, brought calamity wherever he went. There was a black cloud over his head, which followed him everywhere. His name (his identity) was unpronounceable. He was diminutive. He was ugly. He was, to wit, a mirror-image of the illusion produced by believing in one's inner rottenness.

Disease and death are our just deserts. Any time we move closer to these, our guilt lessens, but our anxiety heightens, because we begin to believe the dark side of us cannot be finally destroyed; it is we and we are it.

The depravity illusion makes us suppose that our desires are made of this innate evil, and it all becomes threatening, terror producing, for us. This is the grand illusion, the rider of the white horse, ". . . and he went out conquering and to conquer"(Revelation 6:2), causing the suffering and the agony demanded by a humanness that is basically evil, full of hate and hostility.

When we give up the illusion, when we no longer need it, when we finally discover that it is the illusion, and not we, that is demonic, we begin to realize that our wants, desires, and dreams are actually our "out," the way to close the door on our "evil." They are signs of the inner self, struggling for life, the new life: the life of participation, the life of joy, the life of hope, the life of realization.

It is this new life Jesus came to proclaim and to enable us to find. In forgiveness, the door is shut on evil of our past—finally, completely. We are called toward, and move into, the reality of ourselves and give up the illusion of our essentially evil nature. The hold of the past (I suppose this to be Spangler's racial memory) is broken and we are set free. We are not excused from bad deeds alone, but from an oppressive attitude that has imposed upon us the illusion of our core rottenness.

To sum up: There is an illusion that has come upon some of us. It has been a demonic myth passed on from one generation to another. It is told with threats and fears, with taboo and demand. The end of the illusion is the ultimate threat—hell. The suffering that goes on and on for eternity.

To avoid the ultimate catastrophe, we must give assent to a theology that points us out as rotten at the core and incapable of any good. We spend our life in lemonade limits, never quite breaking into the wine of the Spirit. Wants are to be held suspicious and capable of producing the darkest sins, since they spring up from deep within the "rotten" core.

But such self-rejection is not the thrust of the Bible. God loves, above all else, this creature who shares the Divine Image. God becomes the Divine Lover, seeking to be a part of the life of us creatures and making us part of God's life. God is for freeing us all from whatever oppresses us and from whatever denies us the fullest expression of ourselves. That freedom is called redemption, and Jesus is the model of all of its possibilities, the fulfillment of the forgiveness that frees us from our past, the inspirer of the hope that enables us to view the future with anticipation.

Freedom, forgiveness, and hope begin within, at the core of us, where wants are born—the core that is good and bad, right and wrong, sometimes funny, sometimes sad, but never simply rotten.

Norman Pittenger said it well: "There is nothing *malem in se* (evil of itself). In biblical mythology, even Satan is one of His creatures."[8]

On Being Bored Out of One's Gourd

Jill sat leaning against the headboard of their bed. She was anxiously twisting strands of her long, blond hair. Her eyes were fixed on the hair, but her mind was focused elsewhere.

Jack sat cross-legged in the corner. He seemed to be bathing his face in an unseen light. His eyes were closed, and his hands rested lightly on his knees, palms up, with the thumbs and forefingers almost touching, as if holding something else unseen.

Their house was an old farmhouse. They had gotten free use of it as part of the pay for Jack's work with the farmer. Their move had been part of their commitment to a simple life-style. Jack was handy with tools and had managed to engineer a fairly livable space for a house as badly run-down as this one. They had worked long hours together, sharing all the work, often getting to bed past one, or whenever one of them gave in to fatigue. All the work did little to change Jack's thin-as-a-rail physique, but Jill, who had a tendency toward plumpness, had lost a considerable amount of weight.

Jack seemed transfixed, drinking in whatever invisible sunlight he felt to be falling upon him. There was a faint, maybe beatific, smile on his face.

Jill kept darting glances at Jack and was becoming impatient. It was dark in Jill's corner of the room, and she felt this darkness inside her.

Jack had gotten into meditation in college days. He had experimented with yoga and T.M. He had been, as it is said, "turned on." There was little that Jack tolerated that he could not embrace with intense enthusiasm. So, when he did the meditation thing, he became a wholehearted devotee. Jill had a wider range of enthusiasm—some cold, cool, warm, hot, but seldom red-hot. She had been converted in the late sixties from an upper middle-class, suburban child to a person of whom she was not too certain anymore.

Jack's eyes began to blink. He moved slightly.

"Jack, we need to. . . ."

His eyes closed. The movement stopped. Jill waited.

Jack was also a convert. In fact, converting was his life-style. He had been a radical on campus with the anti-war parades. Then came the environmentalist stage. The same tactics were transferable to the new movement. Jack had organized the sit-in blocking the main gate at the construction site for the nuclear power plant. For a brief time he had even "made the Jesus scene." When this interest in fundamentalism seemed to put space between him and Jill, Jack cooled his infatuation with the Jesus folk.

Jack began to move again, this time rubbing his eyes and stretching his long, skinny legs. He yawned widely and stretched out his arms, as if to embrace the whole universe. Then his eyes opened and he sat there, looking at Jill.

"Jack, I have to talk. I mean I . . ." Her words trailed off into silence.

"Talk, lover. The body is tired, but the mind is wide awake. I can hear you, I mean *really* hear you." There was a tenderness in his voice, genuine and obvious.

Jill sighed and looked down at the hair-twisting fingers. Her words were soft and almost inaudible, "I'm bored, Jack."

"I'm sorry, Lover, I didn't. . . ."

"Bored! I'm bored, Jack." She forced the words out with more volume. She was staring Jack eye-to-eye now.

Jack got up and came to sit beside her on the bed. He brushed a hair out of her face. Jill closed her eyes as if to gain some inner strength from somewhere. Jack spoke gently, "Tired, maybe. Even discouraged. But, Lover, bored? How could you be . . .?"

"Bored! Damn it, Jack. I'm bored! Inside I'm hurting, hurting because I'm so hungry to be with people who are having fun. Poolside parties. Riding Dancer (the family horse). Buying something really fashionable." She seemed surprised at what she had just said, surprised and hurt.

"Oh, Jack, I'm scared that I'm missing it all, all the really neat experiences."

He embraced her and they each wept for different reasons.

8 Hunger for Experience

"Gusto!" the barrel-chested, hairy-chested, *macho* type said as he lifted his can of beer in the commercial. It all had a now-or-never quality to it. One time around! Get all the gusto you can! Whatever may be said about commercials, the once-around life philosophy of that one can hardly be doubted.

A colleague, writing editorials for a church paper, always ended them with the admonition: "Here or nowhere, now or never."

The word seems to have gotten through to the masses. It would appear that there is a frantic rush for once-in-a-lifetime experience. We live in a sort of frenetic, kinetic restlessness in our search for experience. Whether this is more or less than before, the historians of another time can determine, but it feels as if the pace is, if not madder, at least faster than ever before.

It also feels like an addiction with most of us. It feeds on itself, this hunger for experience, and produces an ever-expanding hunger. It is as if we were whirled about by some power that increases its grip and speed with every spin. What satisfied yesterday is insufficient for today, and the hunger keeps growing into gigantic proportions.

Besides the escalation of the whole thing, there is a further bind: choosing. I vote for the side that says that choices are great. Whatever limits our options robs us of some of our freedom and responsibility. While I'm for options, the once-around-life reality urges me to choose now or the choosing time will be gone.

It was circa 1938 that Miss Mathilde Brown's fourth grade was taken to the Southeastern Fair in Atlanta. Mr. Flem Shivers had made his mattress truck available for our transportation. The excitement made us stop more often than Flem had planned for the hour-long trip. I had a quarter in my zippered pocket. On the way, we talked about the best way to protect our funds from pickpockets. After all, we were going to the big city and we had to think about all those things. The real problem with my quarter did not turn out to be the pickpockets. The real problem was where to spend it. There were 15-cent freak shows, all kinds of 5-cent candies, rides for a dime. I knew that I wasn't going to blow it on one of the girlie shows. That cost the whole quarter. Besides, who wanted to watch all those women take off all their clothes? (What does a ten-year old know?) The other end of the bind was that we had to leave at four o'clock. Time was running out. Once around life!

I must have spent it for something, and I don't remember any regrets. What I remember is the bind: limited resources, multiple choices, time running out—now or never.

Coping with this hunger for experience and all its many options brings us right back to wanting. What do we want? What sort of experiences? What experiences do we want more than anything else? What experiences will enable us to achieve our ends, our *raison d'être?* Choosing is inevitable, even if we choose not to choose. So we have to get in touch with ourselves in such a way as to know what we want.

There is, of course, the choice of no choice. If it is made, it ought, at least, to be a conscious one, made in the awareness of who we are and what we want.

While there is this nervous search for experience for many, there are some who seem afraid, especially of freedom and responsibility. To those who are afraid, the plethora of options is frightening, and such persons want to hide, have someone else choose for them, or close themselves off from a world of experiences that may change them, consume them, or make them evil. What if closing the door on most experiences were the real evil? What if living by fear turned out to be the worst idolatry of all? What if our routines, rituals, and ruts were not actually our protectors, but vicious enemies who had stolen away time and opportunity? Here or nowhere. Now or never.

What is to be made of this extraordinary situation—experiences by the carloads? Entertainment. Learning. Working. Building. It is endless, and these experiences have a way of multiplying.

First, I don't intend to be judgmental about experiences. The no-no people may choose to experience list making. I personally don't find much gusto in that. My guidelines will be simple: if it doesn't hurt anyone, it's a lively option. How to determine the "hurt" is obviously the catch. My guess is that we cannot always be 100 percent certain about that, but it is a place to begin.

Secondly (as you have already guessed), I will tend to encourage experience. After all, I have branded this whole business of wanting an act of faith. It seems just as operative where experience is concerned as where singing "Just As I Am" might be. In fact, "Just As I Am" is where it all begins and ends. And "Just As I Am," my identity, has to do with the sum total of my experiences—the Southeastern Fair, the first girl I ever kissed, and singing over and over, "Just As I Am."

To connect this wanting and experience business more directly with the book of faith, remember the story of the jailer in Philippi? (It's in Acts 16.) Paul and Silas had been put in jail for their preaching. An earthquake came along and so badly damaged the jail that the jailer thought all the prisoners had escaped. But they hadn't, as Paul and Silas pointed out, who were sitting contentedly in their cell, singing "Just As I Am." This really got to the jailer, and he asked them, "Men, what must I do to be saved?" (Acts 16:30). The reply was, "Have faith."

The jailer's question has an ironical twist to it. The Greek word for "save" means several things; among the possibilities is "to be delivered," "to be turned loose," "to be set free." How odd that the jailer should be asking the prisoners what he must do to be turned loose! He had sensed a freedom in Paul and Silas, a freedom he did not know, but which he wanted. "Have faith." It is the leap of faith, as Kierkegaard liked to call it, that makes the deer jump over the wall into a place of uncertainty, but of freedom. Better to be free (saved) than certain. The story has a meaning for those of us who may wonder whether or not life is for experiencing. What must I do to be delivered from the prison of fear? Have faith. Leap the wall!

Wanting, and, specifically, wanting experience, is the urge that leads one to ask: what must I do to be delivered (saved)? So I'm not going to waste time suggesting what experiences are to be avoided.

That would be a rip-off. That little gem is yours. My feeling is that limiting experiences is based more on fear (wanting to get back into the safety of the jail) than on faith. Risky? Yes! But that is the very nature of faith; otherwise it would be called certainty. It would be to conclude that it is better not to have loved than to have risked, been honest, experienced, loved and lost. All of this smacks of anti-trust, not in the good business sense, but in the sense of faithlessness. I like the spirit of the writer of Hebrews. When he reflected on the life of Abraham, he concluded, "He went out, not knowing where he was to go"(Hebrews 11:8). And what experiences Father Abraham had! I am for that attitude. It is risky, restless, ready.

If "What shall we avoid?" is a bad question, perhaps a better one is: Toward what does the experience I want tend? When it is projected out to its logical possibilities, what does the end of it look like? If the gusto philosophy is right—I don't have all the time in the world to decide—then I want to know (as far as possible) if ballooning, for instance, is going to move me closer to becoming what I want to be, what I want to have, what I want to achieve. I want to see if ballooning can be the sort of experience I can reflect on, or if it is just one "whoopee time." "Whoopee time" is a good emotional purgative, and every so often my feelings need regularizing. But "whoopee time" is less important than experiences I can integrate into my being, that become part of me, that change me, that have to do with the way I view life. I think ballooning would be such an experience for me. Someday I'm going to jump over the wall(s) and try it. (Now or never . . . hmmmm.)

Much more down to earth was Tom F. Driver's bathtub experience. When I read his book, I found out that even the everyday experience of bathing can be life changing. As he lay there in the tub in an enjoyable early morning solitude, Driver became conscious of his thighs. He had always hated the word "thigh." It had some mysterious and obscene character for him. As he lay there, examining his own thighs, he realized that his thighs were a symbol of a lack of full self-acceptance. It was these muscles that kept him from planting his feet firmly on the ground. The thighs were a way of denying some of the fullness of life. Driver moved on from this immersion experience to claim experience as the source of our encounter with God and with ourselves.[1]

Experiences on which we can reflect, ponder, muse—even thighs in a bathtub—become integral parts of our believing, of our being delivered, saved.

What sorts of experiences are these? In this frame of reference, just what does experience mean?

John E. Biersdorf, from whose book I have borrowed the title of this chapter,[2] offers a definition of experience. This definition provides guidelines for his study of experience. With some modification, I will go with his guidelines for the purposes of this chapter.

1. Experience is some external happening that stimulates a response within me that has something more than passing significance. It is not going to the door to pick up the mail, unless in that happening something from the whole affair calls up some response that says (for instance), "This is no ordinary thing. There is a letter here from IRS!"

2. Experience will have meaning in itself without having to be related to what happened yesterday or to the economy or to music I'm listening to now. Experience will come with a meaning that depends only on itself.

3. Relatedness of the experience will come by interpretation—what I have called reflecting, pondering, musing. The interpretation may be from a simple "it was fun," without any further tinkering with it, to complex and symbolic interpretations.

4. Experience will generate power, energy, force. I get used by Mrs. Blossomton to do some chore she doesn't want to do. I buy all her manipulating sales talk. I agree. Then it hits me with an undeniable force: I've been had. The experience generates the energy of anger, and I have to find a way to release that energy. Experiences with meaning have power they unleash within us. Haven't we sometime or other judged an experience as a "powerful experience"?

Let's move on to look at some categories of experience. Without any attempt to be complete, we can perhaps get some better feeling for our own experiences and of our wanting or not wanting them as we see them in different levels. To corral all kinds of wild, wonderful herds of experience in one enclosure is a larger job than this chapter envisions. My purpose will be, rather, to look at some experience-types that seem especially to excite desiring, wanting.

First of all, there are sensual experiences, some of which meet the criteria we have borrowed from Biersdorf. These are those experiences that come to us through our senses that have an effect on us that is more than a passing interest; that are meaningful within themselves, primarily where usefulness is concerned; that are liable to be interpreted, mused over, pondered; and that generate power and energy within us.

Taste.

All one has to do is to finger-walk through the Yellow Pages to realize that, in most metropolitan areas, all sorts of tasting experiences are available: Moroccan, Italian, Swedish, Chinese.

Newspapers and magazines keep a stream of recipes flowing to spice up the family fare. Variety does spice up life.

The new fad seems to be searching for purity through eating. What sells now is natural food without preservatives, food grown in natural fertilizers.

If one were Freudian, he or she might wax eloquent about the oral meaning of the hunger (sorry for the pun) for taste—back to the breast and all that.

I suspect that taste has a sacred and sacramental value. It hardly matters whether or not it is within the ritual of some church. Taste is not so good alone; it is meant to be shared. Bread broken alone is more bitter than bread shared. It is communion in the most literal sense of that word, a communicating experience. The taste shared, the food enjoyed together, talked about, compared, savored, becomes the experience.

Sound.

What a cacophony of noise we urban Americans endure! It is half-past April, and I am sitting here on the outskirts of Kansas City with the windows open. Some mechanic has dropped a wrench at the local service station. My daughter is buzzing around in the kitchen, with flurries of pot-and-pan sounds. The heavy afternoon traffic whirs by with an occasional horn blast. The news is on the radio. There is a welcome twitter of the birds outside. Someone's dog is complaining, and a kid has just screamed. What does all this experience mean to me? What is it doing to me?

We almost come unglued without all the noise. Soundproof rooms tend to disorient us. Last night a young balloonist said that his first sensation after he had gotten up was the obvious silence. "It was as if someone had pulled my ear drums out," he said. It took some getting used to; then he indicated that it became almost an addiction.

With all our sound, it seems as if meaning through experience of sound has to be screamed, shouted, blasted into us. We dive into discos, where the beat is pounded into the experience seekers.

They seem not so much to be dancing as *bathing* in the sounds that are almost tactile. Perhaps the disjointed sounds are reflections of our feelings about our discordant lives. Is it a ritual to affirm our alienation, sounds so raw and hard that no communion can happen between dancers?

Sounds do create experiences and sometimes bring us to feel and become profoundly aware of what our lives mean or do not mean in this confusing sea of sound. Samuel Miller, late dean of the Divinity School at Harvard, told of his experience of Stravinsky's "Rite of Spring." He much preferred the "Pastoral Symphony" of Beethoven. The sounds were familiar and comfortable. One was certain of where the music was going; it could be accurately anticipated. It went where it was supposed to go. There was symmetry to it. But the "Rite of Spring" was unpredictable. Its chords were strange and disturbing. It lacked symmetry and balance. It required that you focus on what it was saying. It was not music to do anything by. It shouted for attention. It demanded purposeful following. Dean Miller said he had disciplined himself to listen to it for a whole week. It had to be broken into, cracked open, to produce an experience within the listener. One had to break out of comfortable patterns and be laid open to experience.

It all reminded me of John's revealing words, "He who has an ear, let him hear what the Spirit says to the churches"(Revelation 2:7).

Seeing.

The voracious appetite for experiencing through seeing has become almost an obsession with our culture. We want to see in bright, living color, with scenes wrapped all around us, enhanced by having sounds pouring out from all directions.

Movies and television have provided us with an acceptable voyeurism. We can play the part of the peeping-tom within the cover of our homes. We eavesdrop on love trysts, top secrets of the government, private business deals—whatever the story-makers offer us.

To see, really see, beyond appearances is to exercise something alive that can affect one. To be available to seeing experiences, one can hardly go about with the tunnel vision of blinders. Yet this "really seeing" is selective and excluding. It is to be here and not there, to focus on the budding rose, struggling to develop and unfold, and so to be oblivious to sky, trees, grass, the dozing dog, the angry blue jays. Like ears, one may have eyes and see not and thus experience not.

The sensual experiences of smelling, touching, and perhaps sex could be added to the category of sensual experience. I will deal with touching and sexuality under relationships. (Smelling, perfumers to the contrary, has not been all that much of an experience producer for me. Some others may have found smelling to be a different experience.)

The senses are there, sometimes anesthetized, making us skip over whatever may prick, endanger, hurt us. But the same unfeeling, nonseeing, nonhearing, causes us to miss hilarity, tenderness, beauty. Yet, some missing is inevitable. With all senses completely alive and aware of a whole gamut of stimuli, some choosing is inevitable. It means missing something, but choosing is intentional and therein lies an enormous difference between insensitive missing and choosing the experience for focus and depth.

The second category is excitement. The experience of excitement comes through the senses, obviously, but it is a different kind of hunger that has more intention and purpose to it. It is purposely sought after. It is an identification of self with the unusual, the weird, the thrilling. It is a hunger for a contrived ecstasy. It is a quality of our modern life that has become almost a necessity, a way of coping with tension.

Excitement needs to have an edge of danger to it, at least, to have some questionable outcome. A friend once confided that the particular appeal to motorcycling was the danger involved. "When they get those cycles absolutely foolproof and completely safe, I'll quit and maybe take up sky diving."

One edge of excitement is anticipation. To be able to look forward to something that is promising makes some levels of boredom tolerable.

Somewhere the participation has to be had. Waiting and postponing have limits, and the anticipation alone is not enough. The thrill of the chase, the titillation of the roller coaster, the fascination of dice, the stimulation of the competition, the pandemonium of a celebration give us strong echoes that we are alive, awake, in touch with the drama of living. Perhaps we are really seeking more than all that, something beyond—not other than—a further dimension. Excitement needs to be more than a purgative for the sluggishness of soul we call boredom. It needs to go somewhere, make us different, open up new levels of living. Excitement has the potential of letting us off at a different point than where we paid our fare and climbed aboard.

We arrive again at intention. We determine that excitement will become a means, instead of an end. We choose to force it, to give up experiences that yield meaning. It is to decide that we shall have excitement, but not be had by it.

Relationships are experiences, a category that has the potentiality of both sensuality and excitement. It is a category of experience that is a rich source of meaning. It is both alive and dormant. One does not spend every hour of the day relating. Yet, for working time, sleeping time, apart time, there is some sort of connection, "the tie that binds," as the old hymn has it.

Relationship gets experienced first with some signals of acceptance. As Eric Berne pointed out in *Games People Play,* pastimes are a level of relationship—weather talk, swapping golf yarns, comparing prices. Relationships can stay at such a level for years and years. Whether or not our relationships move from pastime toward something with more investment will depend on willingness to risk, to give of self, to push sharing to some deeper level.

Abraham Maslow felt that acceptance was one of our basic needs, so that before one could grow toward a more complete actualizing of self, he or she had to deal realistically with his or her acceptance needs. It is as if acceptance were of itself an enabler. It is an experience that has power to it, one that affects and changes us.

We parson types are often hoisted up on some imagined pedestal. It is a polite way to keep the reverend at arm's length. The pastor is the holy person of God. He or she probably doesn't sweat. The pastor's marriage is a platonic affair, out of which children are conceived through osmosis. The minister's mind is riveted on the things of the spirit. He or she is as liable to sin as hell is to freeze.

Perhaps it all comes from some vicarious need to have some figure in whom fantasies of purity and goodness, discipline and devotion are incarnated. Maybe it is to tickle one's hope with the dream that all this sanctity and holiness is possible. Whatever. I can only guess at the dynamics which I suspect would have wide ranges of differences in the minds of the fantasizers.

What I do know is how lonely it can be, how cut off from the very adoring people one can feel. Clerical adoration is a way of denying the experience of acceptance, and such denial effectively stops the development of any relationship of honesty and openness.

From nervous and unsure acceptance, the experience of relationship can move toward intimacy, which is not some ultimate station of arrival on the friendship line. It is a quality of time that has the most profound meaning people can share. It is a for-the-moment happening. While it is the experience of the depth of relationship, it will not always be the character of every meeting of those who have known the experience of honesty, caring, giving, and receiving—of all that intimacy may involve.

I share myself more completely with people on some occasions than on others. I have never found a fountain of pure intimacy that can be turned on. Sometimes the times aren't ripe. Sometimes I am hiding, looking out through tiny slits in my being that hardly even reveal my eyes' color. I don't always know the reason. But my collection of experiences of high honesty, risky revelation, and unashamed show of feelings remind me of a capacity for intimacy, and, suddenly, I am hungry for the experience again.

It is here, with this sort of depth level of relationship, that I want to deal with touch and sexuality as components of intimacy.

I find the experience of touch sometimes frightening, sometimes consoling, sometimes disagreeable, sometimes sexy, sometimes with no meaning at all. There are obviously all sorts of tactile experiences. Some identify cold, heat, sharpness, smoothness. Some tell if the material is too thick. Some, for those with the discipline and training, enable them to read Braille. There's a wide gamut of touch experiences, but these are information gatherers. I want to deal with the experiences of people touching people. It is this kind of touching that means something, that changes people, that leaves them sometimes wondering "What did that mean?", that caresses and says, "I belong to you."

There are perhaps those who touch others with ease and naturalness. I haven't found it either easy or natural. For a lot of my living, I have kept safe distances. Hand shaking has always been okay, although I remember being obsessed over how long to hold on and how tight to squeeze. In college days my shyness lost me a possible mate. When I finally summoned—God only knows where from—the courage to "pop the question," her reply melted me right into the ground, like hot grease on the sands: "Do you think I want to marry a guy who only knows to hold hands?" Ouch!

Touch is always sexual. It is not always step one toward the bedroom. But from hand shaking to embracing, I have never suddenly become asexual. I am aware of my maleness and of the sexuality of whomever I touch. I still remember the old Emily Post rule: it's okay to offer my hand to another man, but I should wait for the woman to offer her hand.

I touch others with my male body; they touch me with their male or female body. I am always conscious of both touching and being touched. I've come to accept that awareness as OK. It all has to do with who I am, who they are. To deny all that has to do with hiding again, with playacting, perhaps with calculated phoniness.

While I experience touch as sexual, it is more than that. It is sometimes an expression that words can't handle.

John had become a good friend quickly. It seemed from the beginning that we shared the same sorts of values. It was easy to talk to John, because I felt that he heard me in ways more meaningful than just word messages. John was pastor of an experimental church. It was not the run-of-the-mill kind of congregation, obviously. They were applying for membership in our association. I felt it would be an uphill battle; I had not realized how steep the hill would be. After hours of emotional debate, the vote denied John's church membership. I felt crushed, angry, ashamed. I walked over to John, took a long look, and embraced him. Touching said to John what I had no words to express.

The TA (transactional analysis) folk talk of stroking. There is a kind of symbolic touching, a sort of soul-nourishing experience. I suppose that is what is involved in the expression, "I was really touched by what was said." That's got to be on the positive side. But I want, in addition to symbolic stroking, skin-to-skin touching, which, if genuine, beats all I know for saying, "I care about you."

That is some tremendous experience.

So is bedroom touching.

Making love has the potentiality of being the way of experiencing another person totally. It is not always such a total experience. It is also simply a method of relieving gonadal pressures. It can be the soul and body meeting of two people completely lost in the full sharing of each other. Sexual sharing then becomes that sort of experience that has to do with one's most profound values, for sex is—when it is what it can be—the mutual valuing of one another as persons. Such sex has the quality of being a cherished memory to be celebrated and remembered. It is, as Bishop Pike (among others) used to say, a sacrament, which must inevitably mean finding, interpreting, and sharing its meaning.

It is of such sexual encounters of the intimate kind that Rosemary Haughton wrote. She understands the experience of sex as being the experience whereby one comes to know one's self, to experience one's self as a person. Even though the experience of intercourse has to do with union, with oneness of soul and body, it is nonetheless, the experience that reflects one's own uniqueness. It is, after all, this uniqueness that is offered to one's partner, and Haughton concludes that sexual intercourse establishes one's individuality.[3] But is this not like saying that one discovers identity within relationships and that the most profound and complete relationship leads to the most profound and complete discovery of one's self?

The final category I want to deal with is that called "spiritual." I find it a struggle to define "spiritual." On the one hand, it is meant to be quite above and beyond one's ability to confine with words; on the other, it can become so nebulous and ghostly as to mean practically nothing. It is sometimes taken to mean the pious life as over against the "worldly" life. In this sense, "spiritual" usually means something that is nonsensual. As if the sensual, worldly experiences could not possibly be spiritual. I believe the spiritual life can be both sensual and worldly. Without mounting some complicated theological argument, I am suggesting for this discussion that "spiritual" means that dimension of our being that begins with our senses and the world they touch and reaches out into limitless space and eternity.

I have come, rather recently, to this extraordinary dimension of my being. The beginnings of this new entry are back there in the past. Some memories call to mind the fact that all along the way there have been glimpses of this meta-reality—some fledgling attempts to be in communion with an "Other"; the consciousness of some "Presence," which undoubtedly I understood in the words and symbols of my upbringing in the deep South. I have always been drawn to and fascinated by what Rudolph Otto called the *mysterium tremendum,*[4] but my expressions for It then were those of my Baptist and Presbyterian backgrounds.

There were times when I was practicing meditation, but I had no idea that that was the name for it. There was a fireplace in my room. After struggling with homework, I'd turn out all the lights, put on a record from the Carmen Suite, and just let images form in my mind. They had no quality of time or space to them, and anything was possible.

That was nearly thirty-five years ago. Last year I began a serious study of meditation. It was not one of those academic affairs, encountering books and lecturers. It was experiential. My first experience was a deeply emotional encounter with my own spirituality.

My teacher (guru? therapist?) had put the stereo earphones on me and directed me to lean back in the recliner chair. After some relaxation suggestions, she sat in front of me and took down, verbatim, the images I described to her. The music, at first, was soft and flowing. It built to a climactic crescendo and settled in a rich baritone solo. I'll share at this point from her notes:

> The singing is behind me. It is like the man is supporting me, he is behind me and his arms are outstretched. It is almost like I am facing one direction, but I am seeing him behind me. In front, there is a very soft gold light. I think I am lying on his chest. He is a big strong man and he is holding me. It is like he is a protector. Now he is moving away, softly, quietly. Now, he is some distance behind. He is telling me something—some kind of advice—encouragement. I can't understand the words. Now he is gone.
>
> Someone else has come behind me . . . He is smaller than the other man. I think I am that man. I just see a silhouette. It feels good to be that man. I always wanted to sing. It is Betty [my wife, who died in 1964]. She is playing the piano.

At that point I began to weep. I let it go without trying to control it. The session ended shortly after this. I felt exhausted, drained, and strangely alive, aware, wide awake. I don't make any claims as to the "reality" or fantasy nature of what I saw. I do claim it was for me no common dream; it was a spiritual experience, one that touched the deepest values in my life, one to ponder and try to interpret, one that contained within it a meaning of no cheap value.

Hunger for experience in our times has an obvious spiritual dimension to it. Religions of the esoteric East bring a dimension of mystery to their seekers. New religions bring a claim for discipline and sacrifice. Some are good, some bad, some liberating, some oppressing, some joyous, some tragic. One can hardly miss this craving for spirituality by whatever definition.

What shall we make of our hunger for experience?

Obviously, I opt for finding food for our hunger, experiences that are concerned with the deeper levels of our lives, that are meaningful within themselves without leaning on some other structure for meaning, that can be interpreted and shared, that can unleash pent-up sources of power within one's life. There are, of course, experiences that are destructive, bad, maybe even evil. All of which is to say—those sorts of experiences are risky. Sometimes the risk is significant. But I cannot count that risk as reason to deny satisfying the hunger for experience. To guard against experience, to hide it in familiar rituals, is to deny oneself life. And to suppose that such denial is to follow Jesus' dictum about self-denial is to miss the whole point.

Could it not be that the denial that Jesus was talking about was that of the existence lived under the demand of safety first, no risk? It would, after all, fit the context in which he spoke of risking one's life for his sake and that of the Good News.

Jesus spoke of his gift to the believing world as that of eternal life. It has often been supposed to mean time piled on top of time, years stretching into centuries, centuries into millennia and so on. Paul Tillich wrote of eternity, not so much as length of time, but depth, quality of life. The real eternity is now.

Experience has to do with aliveness, with being aware—not merely well informed—but open to the moment, to its possibilities. It is to choose and pursue the hungers that offer the most fulfillment.

Experience is where the rubber hits the road. It is our encounter with reality.

Tom F. Driver has a daring theology of experience. Experience, he suggests, is for us the Word of God. Whatever one accepts as the Word of God—Jesus, the Bible, the pope, the church—that individual has had to determine that it is the Word of God for him or her. How has it been determined? Largely by experience—an experience of teaching/learning, or threatening, or promise—whatever. Experience with the Bible, having to tote it to church at every gathering, taught me that this was God's Word. Without the experience, the interpretation, the sermons, the Sunday school lessons, it might have been the black book with Shakespeare language. No experience—no Word of God. How far wrong is it, then, to say that experience *is* the Word of God?

Experience was surely the word of God for the biblical writers. Especially for the prophets. "The Word of God came unto me saying. . . ." In the midst of life within its own experiences, men met the Lord God and recorded it as such. Driver says:

> I believe that the varied plentitude of our experiences provides the clue to their ethical and religious meaning. Briefly, it is this: the moral and religious life requires that we gather our myriad experiences into significant stories, until life acquires pattern. So also our countless primary experiences represent the encounter of life with life, making patterns where chaos was.[5]

Out of the chaos that was primeval, the Lord God called into order the universe. It was beginning time. Creation, we have called it. But the point is missed about the creator God if one supposes that the act of creation is done, a moment lost in geological eons. The God who calls order from chaos, patterns from confusion, meaning from vacuum's void is the living, changing God we encounter in our own experience.

It is, then, an encounter with God who is not in the nether-nether world of spacial obscurity but is present in the world, still creating, forming, making, and we persons are part of all that activity. Driver's phrase for it is "radical immanence." It is not the pantheism that romantically saw God's presence in the white lily, the dark of night, the rock, the stream, the grass, the fall's red leaves. That was a god hiding in the atom's nucleus. By "radical immanence," Driver means the presence of the Lord God in every experience of us all, our birthing and dying, our fighting and fearing, our loving and our caressing, our working and our playing. The experiences and God have a unity we cannot pull apart. God sees our selling, feels our hurting, smells our sweating, reads our writing, tastes our eating, sits in our meeting. It is not that God is simply ubiquitous Presence. God is not simply pure being (whatever in the world that may be). God is acting, doing. Not only is God present at our selling, hurting, sweating, etc., but also God *is* selling, hurting, sweating, etc.

This God who is in our experience as active participant, Driver points out, is a person, one with whom identity is possible. Such identifying with God is not so much some choice we may have; it is rather a choice God has made. With us, this God too struggles for wholeness and unity.[6] This experiencing of life—the full gamut of it—became human, or in John's sublime words: "The word became flesh and pitched His tent along with ours" (John 1:14, author's paraphrase).

It is the symbol of the tabernacle in the wilderness, the God who chose to identify completely with people. This God determined to take on their bewilderment, their confusion, their death, their struggle, their pain, their sorrow. The tabernacle was the sign of the God who comes to real, live people to live, to act, to fight, to love, to redeem.

It is Isaiah's Immanuel, the Lord God's promise to the prophet as a sign of grace. Immanuel is God with us. It is such a God Yahweh chose to be. God is not simply in our history. That all seems so distant, albeit glorious and theologically sound. The Lord God is in our moments, crises, hassles, in our experience, the whole of it.

If God is present in our experiences, then it is our experiences that bring us into the presence of the Almighty Lord God of heaven and earth. Our experiences are the very word of God. Interpreting those experiences then is to gather them as the stories of our lives, the patterns that become for us the meanings that have the clue to our own purpose.

Wanting experience, in the last analysis, is to want God, for it is there that he is to be met.

There is a reality, Freud taught us, of which we are not conscious. That dark and unknown land is in our ego, our superego, and our id. It sometimes surfaces in dreams, in slips of the tongue, in body language. The whole point of psychoanalysis is to claim as our own more and more of that unexplored land so that life becomes more and more our own possession, wrenched from the unconscious.

To be unaware of meanings within life is to store some valuable part of ourselves in that locked room of unknown dimensions, and that is to lose it. To be unaware of God in our experiences is to lose the sense of another with Whom we share everything.

Ludwig B. Lefebre, in his provocative article in *Psychology Today,* states that psychotherapy, even when it is most successful, still lacks an important dimension, that of enabling a person to experience "extra human partnership." Referring to God, Lefebre wrote:

> He can . . . be experienced as a partner who leaves all responsibility for individual actions to man without judging him. Then punishments and rewards cease to be relevant and are replaced by support, sustenance, and acceptance. This possibility of partnership exists, in my opinion,

> within the Christian context. God-incarnate appears as *the* intermediary, with whom brotherly equality is possible.[7] (Emphasis, Lefebre's)

Experience is God's word for us, and "word," *logos,* is more than the smallest unit of verbal communication. It is "idea," "expression," "statement," "story," "matter," "reason," "affair," "cause." And, as Driver adds, *logos* is shape, Gestalt, pattern. All of these are experiences, and our experiences are the ground of our encounter with the "extra human partner," the Word become flesh, the Lord God.[8]

Wanting, desiring, hungering for experience at its deepest level can be the act of faith by which we seek God. The experiences begin to etch out a pattern, a story, a cohesive whole. Driver called these "patterns of grace."

What shall we say then? Shall desire increase that grace may abound? By all means!

Experience is good, and the hunger for it is an inner insistence that we seek this good, and the chief good of it is that it at once makes us more human and more liable to encounter God.

Here's to experience!

Experience is to feel, to sense, to have all the senses of us
  come alive.
It is to feel danger,
  to feel self impressing itself on and onto others,
  to be urged to respond.
It is to feel your body pressed to muscle-and-bone limits
  thereby setting off fatigue's own exhilaration.
It is to be whisked from the ordinary, the known, the familiar,
  into the unpredictable.
It is to hear, not just out-sounds,
  but sounds that have power to pound themselves into
  one's very marrow.
It is not much for avoiding what is merely unpleasant.
  It is an urgent desire to taste, smell, see . . .
It is to be sometimes "ecstasized"
  caught up in an experience
  having given up compulsive controls.
It is to laugh,
  become a clown, and thrill over the laughter
  of those who experience you as funny.

It is to test your own reality by your antics
    and be affirmed by the laughter.
It is to be in,
    to enter,
    to be surrounded by whatever stimuli there are
    to make you feel alive,
    vibrant, electric.
It is to experience purity,
    probably the purity of your self
    scrubbed free of caked-on inhibitions,
    a kind of basic simplicity—no additives,
    the down-to-earthness—
    the essential and primal identity with earth
    whose dust you are.
It is to know and imitate the ways of nature.
It is to eat and call good
    all the simple fare of whatever is the
    sweet purity of itself
    without the harsh intrusions of potions and mixtures.
    It is to chew and feel the rough grains of the fields.
It is to love so that your self incorporates into itself
    the whole of the experience:
    the ecstasy and the sublimity,
    the pain and the grief,
    the whole and the fractured,
    the guilt and the grace.
It is to live,
    but to live as if there were more.

Notes

Chapter 3

[1] Erik H. Erikson, *Childhood and Society,* rev. ed. (New York: W. W. Norton & Company, Inc., 1963); *Identity and the Life Cycle* (New York: International Universities Press, 1959).

[2] Martin Buber, *Between Man and Man,* trans. Ronald Gregor Smith (Boston: Beacon Press, 1955).

[3] See discussion by Edith Weigert in *Courage to Love* (New Haven, Conn.: Yale University Press, 1970), pp. 189-199.

[4] Paul Tillich, *Dynamics of Faith* (New York: Harper & Row, Publishers, Inc., 1957).

[5] See discussion of Adlerian psychology by Leslie D. Weatherhead, *Psychology, Religion, and Healing,* rev. ed. (Nashville: Abingdon Press, 1952), pp. 267-276.

[6] Thomas Harris, *I'm OK—You're OK: A Practical Guide to Transactional Analysis* (New York: Harper & Row, Publishers, Inc., 1969).

[7] Paul Tillich, *Systematic Theology,* Vol. II, *Existence and the Christ* (Chicago: The University of Chicago Press, 1957), p. 52.

[8] "O World, Thou Choosest Not the Better Part," in Walter Blair and W. K. Chandler, *Approaches to Poetry* (New York: Appleton-Century-Crofts, Inc., 1935), pp. 343-344. Used by permission of Charles Scribner's Sons.

Chapter 4

[1] Dean M. Kelley, *Why Conservative Churches Are Growing* (New York: Harper & Row, Publishers, Inc., 1972).

[2] Sam Keen and Richard L. Critz, "An Interview with Sam Keen on Leaving the Church," *Your Church,* vol. 21, no. 1 (January–February, 1975), p. 61.

[3] Sidney B. Simon, Leland W. Howe, and Howard Kirschenbaum, *Values Clarification: A Handbook of Practical Strategies for Teachers and Students* (New York: Hart Publishing Company, Inc., 1972), p. 19.

[4] Harry Levinson, *The Great Jackass Fallacy* (Boston: Harvard University, Division of Research, Graduate School of Business Administration, 1973), pp. 10-11.

Interlude

[1] David Spangler, *Towards a Planetary Vision* (The Park, Forres, Scotland: The Findhorn Foundation, 1977), pp. 50-59.

[2] Jack Stillinger, ed., *The Poems of John Keats* (Cambridge: Harvard University Press, 1978), p. 372. © 1978 by the President and Fellows of Harvard College. Reprinted by permission.

Chapter 5

[1] William Irwin Thompson, *Passages About Earth: An Exploration of the New Planetary Culture* (New York: Harper & Row, Publishers, Inc., 1973), p. 11.

[2] Frederick Ferré, *Shaping the Future: Resources for a Post-Modern World* (New York: Harper & Row, Publishers, Inc., 1976), p. 1.

[3] *Ibid.,* p. 19.

Chapter 6

[1] Harvey Katz, *Give! Who Gets Your Charity Dollar?* (Garden City, N.Y.: Anchor Press/Doubleday, 1974), p. ix.

[2] Vance Packard, *The Waste Makers* (New York: David McKay Company, Inc., 1960).

[3] Eric Berne, *Games People Play* (New York: Grove Press, Inc., 1964).

Chapter 7

[1] George Park Fisher, *History of Christian Doctrine* (New York: Charles Scribner's Sons, 1898), p. 185.

[2] Henry Bettenson, ed., *Documents of the Christian Church* (New York: Oxford University Press, 1947, 2nd edition 1963), p. 345. © Oxford University Press 1963. Used by permission of Oxford University Press.

[3] Quoted by Charles Augustus Briggs, *Theological Symbolics* (Edinburgh: T. & T. Clark, 1914), p. 376.

[4] John Murray, "Depravity," *Twentieth Century Encyclopedia of Religious Knowledge* (Grand Rapids: Baker Book House, 1955), p. 331.

[5] John M. Krumm, *The Art of Being a Sinner* (New York: The Seabury Press, Inc., 1967), p. 56.

[6] Paul Ricoeur, *The Symbolism of Evil* (New York: Harper & Row, Publishers, Inc., 1967), pp. 35-36.

[7] David Spangler, *Towards a Planetary Vision* (The Park, Forres, Scotland: The Findhorn Foundation, 1977), p. 22.

[8] From a lecture delivered at St. Paul's School of Theology, Kansas City, 1976.

Chapter 8

[1] Tom F. Driver, *Patterns of Grace: Human Experience as Word of God* (New York: Harper & Row, Publishers, Inc., 1977), pp. 3-28.

[2] John E. Biersdorf, *Hunger for Experience: Vital Religious Communities in America* (New York: The Seabury Press, Inc., 1975).

[3] Rosemary Haughton, *The Theology of Experience* (Paramus, N.J.: Newman Press, 1972), pp. 134-136.

[4] Rudolph Otto, *The Idea of the Holy,* trans. John W. Harvey (London: Oxford University Press, 1923), pp. 12ff.

[5] Driver, *op cit.,* p.144.

[6] *Ibid.,* p. 153.

[7] Ludwig B. Lefebre, "Human and Extra-Human Partnership," *Psychology Today,* November, 1968, p. 63.

[8] Driver, *op. cit.,* pp. 145-146.